# The First Session
# with Teenagers

# Neil G. Ribner

Jeanne Albronda Heaton
*Series Editor*

# The First Session with Teenagers

## A Step-by-Step Guide

Jossey-Bass Publishers
San Francisco

Jossey-Bass books and products are available through most bookstores. To contact Jossey-Bass directly, call (888) 378-2537, fax to (800) 605-2665, or visit our website at www.josseybass.com.
Substantial discounts on bulk quantities of Jossey-Bass books are available to corporations, professional associations, and other organizations. For details and discount information, contact the special sales department at Jossey-Bass.

 Manufactured in the United States of America on Lyons Falls Turin Book. This paper is acid-free and 100 percent totally chlorine-free.

**Library of Congress Cataloging-in-Publication Data**

Ribner, Neil.
  The first session with teenagers: a step-by-step guide / Neil G. Ribner.—1st ed.
      p.  cm.
  Includes bibliographical references and index.
  ISBN 0-7879-4982-5 (acid-free paper)
  1. Adolescent psychotherapy.   2. Teenagers—Mental health.   I. Title.
RJ503 .R53 2000
616.89'14'0835—dc21                                                          99-006908

FIRST EDITION
*HB Printing*   10 9 8 7 6 5 4 3 2 1

# Contents

*To Matt, Lauren, and Jason*
*Who taught me what it's really like to be an adolescent*
*and who, by being great kids, allowed me to be a good father*

# Foreword

Much has changed over the thirty years that I have been a clinician, supervisor, teacher, and student of psychotherapy. Therapy is briefer, more people have access to help, psychotropic medications are more effective, and the stigma associated with psychological help has decreased.

One issue, however, remains constant: therapists have always known that the first session is crucial for both emergency intervention and beginning the process of change. Current mental health practice, moreover, renders the first session even more preeminent, since managed care and insurance benefits are limited and the nature of treatment has focused more on problem solving and short-term goals. In fact, 40 percent of all psychotherapy clients today attend only a single session, and the rest typically have four or five meetings.[1]

As therapists we know that we must use the first session to:[2]

- Establish a relationship and working alliance

- Assess the need for crisis intervention

    Evaluate presenting problems and establish a diagnosis

    Explore emotions

Focus the problem(s)

Reach mutual agreement on what needs to be done

- Explore options for solution (one of the alternatives may be to continue therapy)

Consequently, the First-Session Series has been launched with full appreciation for the magnitude of accomplishing these goals in a single session. Likewise, this series is also intended to demonstrate sensitivity and respect for the diversity of background, culture, and experience of clients we hope to serve.

Much can be said for the generic skills necessary for a successful first session, but most therapists are aware of the necessity of customizing our interventions to the specific needs of our clients. What we need to know for a successful first session with a teenager may be very different from what we need to know for a septuagenarian. Consequently, this series provides students, educators, and practitioners with essential knowledge of how to enrich existing therapeutic skill with specific information fine-tuned to meet the demands of diverse populations.

Because adolescents are usually ambivalent, often baffled, but nonetheless resolute in the conviction that they know how "IT" is, they present special challenges for therapists during a first session. Dr. Ribner helps us negotiate a path that both meets ethical guidelines and anchors the therapeutic relationship with enough rapport to accomplish necessary changes. Using humor, intelligence, and compassion, Dr. Ribner guides us through successful first sessions with both teenagers who have normal development issues such as discovering identity, establishing intimacy, and cultivating competence, and teenagers who have serious mental health problems such as substance abuse, eating disorders, delinquency, depression, and violence.

Dr. Ribner's years of experience are reflected in his detailed descriptions of how to integrate the family, the court system, physicians, school personnel and other tangles to the web surrounding the adolescent. Throughout this book, he brings to life the perspective of the adolescent that is the prerequisite awareness therapists need for a successful first encounter.

Discovering how their basic therapeutic skills must be adapted to meet the needs of adolescents is likely to inspire therapists to learn more about enhancing the effectiveness of their first sessions with other populations they serve. Upcoming titles in this series will provide the culturally competent direction necessary to facilitate first sessions with other groups that also require special sensitivity, including older adults, substance abusers, and African Americans. With each new book in this series, we hope to instill not only greater understanding of your clients as a special group but also more compassion for the unique qualities of each individual.

Finally, we hope that the wisdom, experience, techniques, and strategies our authors present will enhance the overall effectiveness of each first session.

*December 1999*                                Jeanne Albronda Heaton
*Athens, Ohio*

# Acknowledgments

I'd like to express my appreciation to the many people who have contributed to my knowledge of adolescents over the years. My sincere gratitude goes to my first mentors at Ohio University—Jim Gleason and Fred Weiner—whose experience and support helped me gain immeasurable confidence, and whom I am proud to call friends. I want to thank another friend and colleague from Ohio University, Jeanne Heaton, who asked me to do this book and whose editorial comments were invaluable.

I am also very grateful to the staff and interns at Social Advocates for Youth in San Diego, who have challenged me over the past fifteen years with some of the most difficult and many of the most rewarding cases with which anyone can imagine working. My sincere thanks also to my partner in private practice for many years, John Reis, who was always available for a consult, a hug, or a pat on the back.

My work at the California School of Professional Psychology since 1978 has been intensely gratifying. I am thankful to all my graduate students and interns who have kept me on my toes and have often been more my teachers than my students. I feel very lucky to have as my boss and close friend Don Viglione, who has been instrumental in supporting my professional development and is always there to share his wisdom. And many thanks to Sandra

Foulds for encouraging my work on this book as well as my other professional ventures.

Most of all, I want to express my thanks from the bottom of my heart to my family, who put up with me throughout my writing of the book and who always keep me grounded: Lewis, Michelle, Mom, and especially my wife, Linda, whose love sustains me.

*December 1999*                                                    Neil G. Ribner
*San Diego, California*

# Preface

I wrote this book to share my thirty years of experience in working with adolescents. When I first started graduate school in 1967, I was certain that the focus of my clinical work would be with young people and their families. Although internships and jobs have included considerable work with adults, I've always returned to my first love: children and adolescents.

Therapeutic work with teenagers has not always been pleasant, and certainly not always smooth. Adolescence is a turbulent period, and teens typically act out the turbulence in the sessions themselves. Thus, my own emotions, not to mention my sense of competence, have run the gamut from the highest highs to the lowest lows, sometimes within the course of a fifty-minute session!

Over the years, I've come to recognize the critical importance of the first session with an adolescent. Both in my own work as well as in supervising hundreds of new clinicians, success and failure have often depended on how that initial session was conducted. I now firmly believe that even if someone is a brilliant diagnostician and an outstanding therapist, his or her treatments run the risk of being inefficient and even ineffective if that therapist hasn't engaged the young person at the start.

This book, then, is not about diagnosing teenagers, nor is it about treatment planning or conducting therapy itself; it is about encountering the adolescent during the first session and establishing a working relationship. It is not meant to be read as a cookbook, though my intent is to provide practical and clinically oriented material that will enable you to experiment with your own style.

I have written this book for both novice therapists and experienced clinicians alike, whether you work in a private practice, hospital, outpatient clinic, or juvenile detention center. I am hopeful you will find the book a useful guide in your work with this most challenging population.

# Introduction

I've often thought that all therapists who do therapy with adolescents should, as a prerequisite to their clinical work, spend a portion of their training riding roller-coasters. Although this idea may be stretching the point a bit, all of us who have treated teenagers understand the emotional swings in this work, for adolescence is a tumultuous time, marked by dramatic physical, social, and psychological changes. The teen who is so sweet and cooperative one day looks sullen and bitter the next. Some days, they're on top of the world, expressing the sense of invulnerability that drives parents crazy. Other days, they're silent, sitting with arms crossed, daring us to engage them.

Helping adolescents negotiate the twists and turns of their teen years has been an enormously satisfying professional experience for me. I've been directly confronted by teenagers in ways adult clients wouldn't dream of, and have sometimes been surprised that I've landed on my feet instead of upside down. I've been constantly challenged to think and rethink my approach, because talking with an adolescent isn't the same as talking with another adult. When working with teenage clients, I've had thoughts similar to those I had when my own children were teens: "Will I ever get through this?" "Why is he acting this way?" "Bite your tongue!" "Don't get into a power struggle." "Guide, don't push." "Be here for her but don't intrude."

Maintaining a steady course in the face of the teen's ups and downs can test the patience and skill of even the most experienced therapist. Practitioners not used to working with adolescents can easily get caught in the pushes and pulls and can feel as though they've not made the slightest progress with the young client. Having a sense of what the adolescent needs is not enough, because unless we make the connections during the very first session, we may have no credibility in the young person's eyes. If we don't gain the teen's trust, we are just "along for the ride" and not guiding the process.

Some mistakes I made early in my career illustrate the vital importance of engaging the adolescent in the first session.

---

Lisa was a thirteen-year-old referred by her school for truancy. She was a bright, talkative girl who had no problem describing why she hated school: "School's dumb." "All you do is sit around all day listening to some stupid teacher tell you what to do." "My teacher thinks she knows more than I do—she hasn't got a clue!" "Why should I learn this stuff anyway?"

I let Lisa ramble, because I thought she might react to structure in the therapy setting as she reacted to structure in the classroom. I failed to ask her about her family and how her feelings about school might have reflected any concerns she had about other parts of her life. Lisa ran away from home two days after our initial session.

---

Brent, a fourteen-year-old ninth grader, was brought to therapy by his parents, who worried about his marijuana use. Brent's goal, needless to say, was merely to get his parents off his back, and he insisted that no one could get him to stop smoking weed. I wanted him to know that his parents were just trying to do what they believed was in his best interests, even if he disagreed, and that they had a right to make the rules of the house. Looking back, I can see that even though these points were true, the first session was not the appropriate time for me to take these positions. Brent was dragged to the next two sessions by his parents, who then called to say he didn't trust me and that they were tired of hassling with him; they canceled all future sessions.

---

This book grew out of my experiences with clients like Lisa and Brent, and out of my conviction that we should never underestimate initial therapeutic connections with adolescents. It is in the initial encounter that teens make a decision about us; directly or indirectly, they are asking

Are you trustworthy?

Can you keep secrets?

Do you really understand me?

Are you going to side with my parents?

Are you trying too hard to be "cool"?

Although competence in assessment, treatment planning, and conducting the therapy are of course critical, even the best clinician had better plan for a really bumpy ride if he or she hasn't made an early connection.

My experience has also taught me that our knowledge of how to do first sessions with children can't always be generalized to initial therapeutic encounters with adolescents, because teenagers are no longer children. Certainly there are similarities between children and teens of which we need to be aware and to take into account in treatment planning, such as the fact that almost all minors are brought to therapy because someone else decided the young person needed it. But we need to remember that unlike most latency-age kids, who still depend on their parents' approval, teenagers often don't care that their behavior isn't approved of by others, and they resist our attempts to get them even to acknowledge that a problem exists!

When I think of Brandon, a sixteen-year-old arrested for being drunk in public, I remember the T-shirt he wore to our first session. It said, "I have no alcohol problem—I drink, I pass out, I wake up— no problem!" Many teenagers brought to therapy feel the same way. They may recognize that they drink or use drugs or binge and purge or stay out all night—but they don't think these things are prob- lems. Young teens are by definition egocentric, and they typically believe they are invulnerable to harm; with conviction, they tell their therapist, "I take drugs, but I know I won't get hooked," or "Sure I have unprotected sex, but there's no way I'll get pregnant."

It's so tempting for us as helping professionals to moralize when we hear statements like these. Although this approach might work with younger kids, it won't work with adolescents, because to some degree, that's just what they're waiting for. Troubled teens often feel rebellious and argumentative; it comes with the territory. So if the therapist picks up the gauntlet, both the battle and the war may be over as quickly as they began.

## OVERVIEW OF THE CONTENTS

How then can we conduct effective initial sessions with adolescents? Because the teen years are often tumultuous in and of themselves, it's vital to know what normal teenage behavior looks like so that we can assess whether a young person's behavior is truly problematic or somewhat normal for the age group. I'll discuss normal adolescent development in Chapter One, and review the four major areas: phys- ical, cognitive, and emotional development, and identity formation. In Chapter Two we'll explore how difficulties in normal develop- ment turn into behavioral or psychological problems for teenagers; we will also look at how adolescents present for therapy.

Because first sessions with adolescents are different than those with children or adults, it's important to anticipate and plan for common pitfalls and traps. In Chapter Three I'll discuss special considerations in preparing for the first session with a teenager. We'll explore questions like these: Should you see the teen with his or her parents or alone? What should you say about confidentiality? How formal should you be? How much should you self-disclose? How should you prepare to meet with a teenager from a different culture?

In Chapters Four and Five I'll present my ideas for conducting an effective first session with adolescents. In the first session you must assess key issues in order to ensure a successful outcome; I'll review not only what to look for but how to gather that information in a therapeutic manner. I'll also talk about establishing rapport, framing the problem in a way that the young person can accept, and developing a working contract with the teen.

Although the information I present in the first five chapters is applicable to all teens, there are some groups of adolescents who have special needs. In Chapter Six, I'll discuss working with special populations of adolescents, such as those who have one or more disabilities, who live in divorced families or stepfamilies, or who come from minority cultures. Chapter Seven is a case study, illustrating the principles and techniques covered in the preceding chapters.

---

My fondest hope is that this book will enable you to get off to a good start in your treatment of adolescents. Although the therapy is never easy, I hope that by following some of the suggestions in this book you will feel more potent in your work. Ultimately, doing effective therapy with adolescents will be rewarding and enriching for both you and your clients!

# 1

# Adolescent Development

Children change when they reach adolescence, and their parents are often confused about how to handle these changes. Well-meaning adults worry about whether or not their teenager is normal and about doing the right thing as parents so that the young person turns out OK. For the adolescent as well, the smoothness of childhood seems overnight to become full of rough spots.

> Johnny, age fifteen, doesn't understand why his mother hates his music and is always telling him to turn it down. He's beginning to wonder whether she understands anything about him.

> Thirteen-year-old Vanessa doesn't want to spend time with her parents like she did before, especially if they're going to do all that "dumb stuff" they used to do when she was younger.

> "Whatever happened to free speech?" asks David. "Why do I have to watch what I say in my own house?"

> "My parents live in the Stone Age," says Kevin. "Everyone nowadays has an earring and a tattoo. My parents think they have to keep an eye on me every minute."

> "I'm not a kid anymore!" insists fourteen-year-old Carly. "I'll make my own decisions about where I go and who I go with."

Sound familiar? Parents who have tried to do their best, who have sacrificed for their family, and who actually may have a good relationship with their child suddenly find themselves questioning where they went wrong. The unconditional love they've felt for their youngster is threatened, and these adults feel hurt and angry about the way they're being treated.

> "He acts as if we're from another planet! He doesn't even want to be seen with us anymore," complains the father of a thirteen-year-old.
>
> "I don't know where she learned such language—we certainly don't say such things in our house," proclaims another.
>
> "I thought we had such a good relationship," worries the mother of a fourteen-year-old. "Now she's pregnant and rejecting everything we believe in."
>
> "It's my daughter's attitude we can't stand. She talks back and basically thinks she can do whatever she wants."
>
> "First he gets suspended from school; now he gets arrested for shoplifting. I tried to raise him right—it must be those friends he hangs out with!"

Although at times it seems to parents that either they or their child won't survive the young person's teenage years, obviously most do. As a matter of fact, many of the issues teens or parents present to therapists reflect the normal turbulence of the adolescent years; if the adults maintain their values and don't overreact, the kids usually turn out OK.

Parents can also underreact to their adolescent who really needs help. What starts as picky eating might become an eating disorder. What looks like a need for privacy might turn into isolation and mask a full-blown depression. What begins as a challenge to authority sometimes becomes delinquency. Many of these problems might have been avoided if the family had sought help at the right time.

Much of my clinical work has involved consulting with parents and counselors to help them assess the seriousness of an adolescent's behavior. Critical to this assessment is an understanding of the adolescent's behavior in relation to developmental norms, because behavior that might be abnormal for younger children or adults may not be pathological for teenagers. In fact, some behavior problems are actually a part of normal adolescent development! Acting out, social withdrawal, or mood swings, for example, may not indicate severe pathology in teens, and we should not overdiagnose such behaviors. However, we should not merely dismiss intense emotional turmoil or family problems as a normal part of growing up, because certain assumptions about teenagers may not be consistent with research literature.

Our awareness of expected behaviors thus helps us differentiate minor problems from those that may necessitate clinical intervention. Such knowledge also allows us to plan our interventions and establish treatment goals within a developmental framework—we shouldn't expect thirteen-year-olds to respond to the same treatment strategies or to achieve the same outcomes as eighteen-year-olds! Assessing the developmental level of our young client during the initial session and comparing it to what the literature characterizes as normal for his or her age are the basis of diagnosis and treatment planning.

As we review normal adolescent development, it is important to keep in mind that not all deviations from the norm result from psychological problems. We must also consider biological and social factors when attempting to understand teenagers. Physical or developmental disabilities, childhood illnesses, and early trauma all influence the adolescent's development. Similarly, we should not expect teenagers raised in different cultures to display the same behaviors at the same time as those raised in the mainstream culture.

Although each teenager is an individual with his or her own genetic makeup, early childhood experience, cultural background, personality, interests, and talents, all adolescents go through relatively predictable stages and face similar developmental tasks. The physical, social, and emotional changes teens go through all have psychological ramifications and, if these changes are not dealt with appropriately by the adolescent and his or her family, may result in problems that warrant counseling. In this chapter, I examine these developmental norms, and in Chapter Two I discuss how difficulties in making smooth transitions from childhood to adolescence manifest themselves in presenting problems of teenagers.

For the purposes of our discussion I've broken down adolescent development into four categories—physical maturation, cognitive and intellectual growth, emotions, and identity formation—and describe the tasks that every young person faces in the adolescent years.

# PHYSICAL DEVELOPMENT

Physical maturation brings about a multitude of concerns for teenagers related to bodily changes, nutrition and health, sex, and the use of alcohol, drugs, and tobacco. Some of the crucial decisions for all teens, such as those related to eating habits, dieting, engaging in sex, and the use of substances, are intertwined with the adolescent's identity development, but I have included them in this section because of their physical ramifications.

## Bodily Changes

Toward the end of childhood, biological changes produce growth spurts, changes in physical appearance, and the development of secondary sex characteristics. Over the past century, the age at which puberty begins has decreased, so that girls as young as nine or ten and boys as young as twelve begin to show pubertal changes.

Although pubertal development follows a relatively predictable course, the rate of such development varies from person to person. Thus, in the same middle school class, we see boys with mustaches and deep voices, and boys who still look and sound like children.

We see girls who have begun to develop breasts and body hair and others who are small and flat chested.

Growth spurts also occur at different ages for different kids, so it's not unusual to see young teens in the same class or on the same sports team who are dramatically different in height and body type. Can you picture the six-foot-tall seventh grader who looks like a football player guarding the skinny, tiny kid in a soccer game? And, for a period of several years, girls on average are taller and heavier than boys. Do you remember what kids look like at an eighth-grade dance?

Both early and late physical maturation can present problems for adolescents. Early maturing males may have some social advantages during adolescence—they are often more masculine and more athletic, leading to greater popularity and self-esteem. However, they are also more likely to associate with older boys and may be drawn into delinquent behaviors, truancy, and drugs. Late-maturing males are often attention seeking, rebellious, and dependent. Yet as they get older, these young men often become more flexible and insightful than their peers.

For girls, early maturation may also bring them popularity, but they often are more vulnerable to risky behaviors, such as drug use and sex. They also tend to do more poorly in school, to be delinquent, and to have eating disorders. If these issues are worked through, however, they make good adjustments in adulthood. Late-maturing girls are more likely to have a positive body image and to be more gregarious, poised, and assertive, yet they may be more anxious and have more self-doubt. For both sexes, advantages of early maturation and disadvantages of late maturation may not persist into adulthood, and we should be aware of the high-risk status of adolescents who mature early.[1]

Research shows that it is not early or late maturation per se that creates problems for teens, but rather a combination of factors that include how adolescents views themselves in relation to their peers and how the important people in teens' lives, especially parents, react to those physical changes. Several authors note the moderating effects of others' responses[2] and underscore that we as therapists must take into account the manner in which the family and peers respond to the adolescent's advancing development.[3]

## Body Image

Although teens tend to cope very well with pubertal changes, many become preoccupied with their physical appearance. Taking long showers and spending hours in front of a mirror are not unusual occurrences (although late-maturing boys often have to be bribed to keep themselves well groomed!). Despite parents' reassurances that their teen looks fine, the young person may feel miserable if her hair isn't perfect or if he gets a zit. Adults may need to be reminded that a good part of self-esteem in adolescents is linked to body image, and as therapists we need to be extremely sensitive to the possible impact on self-esteem of how adolescents perceive their looks.

One of the major bodily changes that is agonizing for adolescents is acne. Acne occurs in 80 percent of girls and 90 percent of boys during adolescence, and teens often have significant emotional reactions to it. For example, about one-third of teens with acne say they feel embarrassed or anxious or have low self-esteem due to their complexion, and almost all worry about their skin.

It's also not unusual for adolescents to put on weight or to have certain parts of their body grow out of proportion to other parts, changes that also potentially lead to self-consciousness and self-doubts. Asking teens how they feel about their acne and other aspects of their body may feel uncomfortable for some counselors and certainly may be embarrassing for young clients to discuss, but it is important to bring up these issues, as they could explain some teens' negative self-image and resultant lowered confidence and self-esteem.

Another important reason to ask adolescents for their feelings about their body and the changes brought on by puberty is that not all teenagers have Caucasian standards of beauty as portrayed in fashion magazines. We should never assume that the teenager has a body-image problem based merely on our own observation of the teen's appearance. For example, African American girls are typically much more satisfied with their bodies than are Caucasian girls and do not strive to be ultrathin.

Although as young people mature and the reliance on physical attractiveness for self-esteem decreases, for some young women the problem of body image has long-lasting effects. Some react to bodily changes by developing better eating habits or increasing their physical activity, but others try to lose weight in unhealthy ways. Particularly for girls, preoccupation with body image can lead to attempts at self-starvation or roller-coaster dieting, discussed in Chapter Two.

## Health and Nutrition

Clearly, some of the weight gain during adolescence is related to teenagers' eating habits. Both boys and girls need increases in vitamins and minerals during the teen years, but because boys grow more during adolescence, they need more calories than girls do. It's not unusual to hear parents of teenagers, particularly those of boys, talk about their child eating all day long; I can recall numerous times when my own teens would complain that they were "starving" no more than an hour after having a big meal.

To some teens, a steady diet of pizza, burgers and fries, soda, chips, and other junk foods seems perfectly fine to them, much to the consternation of their parents. Skipping breakfast and then snacking excessively is a common pattern in adolescence and may lead to nutritional deficiencies, anemia, and delays in sexual maturation. We should stay alert to signs of emerging unhealthy or self-destructive dietary patterns.

## Sex

It's probably a safe bet to assume that your teenage client is sexually active, particularly as he or she approaches eighteen years of age. I'll talk later in this chapter about the development of sexual identity, but in this section I want to cover sexual exploration as a normal developmental process of the teen years.

Clearly, the past several decades have witnessed a change not only in what teenagers do sexually but also in their attitudes about their sexual behavior. For example, by the late 1970s, 70 percent of boys and 45 percent of girls under age fifteen admitted to masturbating, a significant increase since the early 1970s.[4] Of course, it's impossible to know whether these statistics reflect an actual increase in behavior or merely more of a willingness to admit it. Nevertheless, masturbation in adolescents is common.

Over the past thirty years, rates for premarital sex have also risen; in 1985, 79.3 percent of college males and 63 percent of college females reported having engaged in sexual activity, up from 65.1 percent and 28.7 percent, respectively, in 1965. In the same study, only 15.9 percent of males and 17.1 percent of females reported believing that premarital sexual intercourse was immoral.[5] In a 1988 study, 33 percent of males and 25 percent of females had experienced sexual intercourse by age fifteen, and 86 percent of males and 80 percent of females had done so by age nineteen.[6]

Many sexually active teens do not use contraception regularly, and most have had intercourse at least once without using any form of birth control. Although the evidence is that contraceptive use is increasing, many teens still run the risk of contracting sexually transmitted diseases (STDs) and of having an unwanted pregnancy. In fact, of the teens who have engaged in sexual activity, one in six has had a STD,[7] and many teens may be HIV-positive and not know it until they get AIDS in their twenties or thirties. More than one million teenagers become pregnant each year, and estimates are that one in five fourteen-year-old girls today will become pregnant before reaching age eighteen.[8]

Why don't adolescents use contraception regularly? Many are ignorant about the biological facts of life. Some teens are embarrassed about getting contraceptives or don't know where to get them. Some believe it diminishes the romantic aspects of sex, and some are afraid to use contraceptive devices or don't plan in advance to have sex. For others, their belief in their own invincibility takes over, and they deny the possibility of disease or pregnancy. I remember talking with a fourteen-year-old girl who tearfully admitted that she didn't think she could get pregnant the first time she had intercourse. Because the research shows that most teens would fail tests of sexual knowledge, it's obvious why there are so many teenage parents and why the rates of STDs in teens are increasing.

## Tobacco

Despite the health warnings about the dangers of tobacco, 27.8 percent of high school seniors smoke regularly; more teenage girls smoke than boys.[9] Research suggests that adult smokers usually took their first puff between ten and twelve years of age and became physically dependent on nicotine by age fifteen.[10]

## Alcohol

Alcohol is the one drug that has shown a decrease in usage by teenagers over the past twenty years; however, alcohol use remains at a very high level. By the mid-1990s, 45.3 percent of eighth graders, 63.5 percent of tenth graders, and 73.7 percent of high school seniors reported drinking alcoholic beverages in the previous year.[11]

## Substance Abuse

Take a guess as to what the third most abused substances are among twelve- to fourteen-year-olds in the United States, right behind alcohol and tobacco. Inhalants! As many as one in five students in the United States has tried inhalants by the time he or she reaches seventh grade, including such common household products as correction fluid, hair spray, paint, and air fresheners. Hundreds of young people die each year from inhalant use, and those who abuse inhalants on a regular basis put themselves at risk for brain damage.

Although the current rate of drug use (excluding inhalants) in adolescents is less than it was in the 1960s and 1970s, substance abuse by teenagers has increased substantially since the early 1990s.[12] An equally alarming statistic is that young people are becoming involved with drugs at an earlier age—surveys indicate that approximately 20 percent of eighth graders have tried marijuana (about double the rate reported in 1991), 4.2 percent have used cocaine (compared to 2.3 percent in 1991), 2.3 percent have used heroin (1.2 percent in 1991), and 13.1 percent have used stimulants (10.5 percent in 1991).[13] Trends for tenth and twelfth graders are similar.[14] Young persons are also indicating decreases in their beliefs about the risks of drug abuse.

The effects of drugs and alcohol are obvious in the teen years and beyond. Many young persons get in trouble through substance abuse, and alcohol use is a contributory factor in sexual behavior and delinquency. The leading cause of death among fifteen- to twenty-four-year-olds is alcohol-related car accidents.[15] Those who began smoking or using drugs in their teen years tend to continue to use these substances into adulthood and have poorer health and unstable job and marital histories. Thus, even though substance use is often seen by developmental psychologists as a part of normal adolescent development, a "rite of passage," early and continued use is problematic.

## INTELLECTUAL DEVELOPMENT

Between the ages of eleven or twelve and fifteen, adolescents begin to think in terms of abstractions and possibilities. Piaget noted that adolescence is the period in which adult-level reasoning begins to take place.[16] Teens can understand that there may be many different reasons for a behavior, and, because they can now think hypothetically, adolescents can consider possibilities, even those that do not exist in real life. Parents are often struck by how their teenager can come up with ideas that are so different from their own and that seem so unfeasible. Yet this abstract thinking is critically important in helping the young person develop a sense of values and ideals.

## Adolescent Egocentrism

Intellectual development also allows adolescents to begin to see the world as others do and to evaluate themselves as they think others will. Because teens are concerned primarily about themselves, they believe that others are focused on them as well. David Elkind has called this inability to differentiate between what one is thinking and what others are thinking *adolescent egocentrism*.[17]

Young teens will often tell me they are convinced that others still remember the "stupid" comment they made last week or would notice if they wore the same outfit again or will talk about them if their hair is out of place. Let's keep in mind that some of this worry may be well founded—teens often make demeaning comments to each other, like, "Uh! That outfit again?!" However, much of the self-consciousness arises from normal adolescent egocentrism.

Out of this egocentrism comes the phenomenon of what Elkind calls the imaginary audience; that is, adolescents believe that they are on stage and everyone else is evaluating them.[18] Now able to think abstractly, the young person is convinced that others see them in the same way they see themselves. Recently I saw a cartoon in which, in the first panel, a teenage cheerleader was complaining to a friend about having a zit; in the second panel, we see her during a halftime routine at the Super Bowl, absolutely sure that now one hundred million people were looking at her and her zit! This self-consciousness may explain the teenager's need for privacy, as a respite from this imagined scrutiny from others.

Another outgrowth of egocentrism is what Elkind calls the personal fable: adolescents believe that their experience is unique and that they are not subject to the rules that govern others.[19] "You just don't understand me" is a constant refrain from teens, who believe that what they are going through is absolutely unique. A seventeen-year-old college freshman once told me on intake that she didn't think even God could understand her problem, which happened to be that she was in love with two boys at the same time!

The personal fable may in part explain adolescent risk taking: teenagers may believe that what happens to others just won't happen to them. I can recall several cases of teens having unprotected sex, certain that STDs or pregnancy is "something that happens to other kids," or of minors being shocked that they actually got caught shoplifting. All parents who have raised teenagers can recall rolled eyes or refrains of "don't worry" after they've told their child to be careful or asked them to read a news article about teenagers who have gotten injured after behaving foolishly. Counselors, too, are often in disbelief that their teenage clients don't acknowledge the risks in their behavior.

Elkind describes other behaviors typical of adolescent egocentric thinking. Because teenagers can now see various perspectives, they may seem to take every opportunity to argue with adults, and they seem compelled to criticize the people they once idealized. I wish I had a nickel for every parent who felt personally hurt by his teen's comments or who complained to me about his child's "attitude problem." Staying out of the name-calling power struggle is difficult for many adults but may be essential for maintaining family harmony.

Adolescents are well known for believing in something one day and believing in something else the next. The concrete choices of childhood are pretty simple compared to the vast number of choices in the teen years, and young people's awareness of multiple perspectives makes it difficult for teens to make up their minds. Adolescents often also seem hypocritical, espousing strong beliefs about an issue but acting in an inconsistent fashion; for example, they may argue with parents about deserving more independence while asking for money so they can go out.

## Academics and Career Choices

As we have seen, early adolescence is a period of rapid physical, cognitive, and social changes. Partly because of the special needs of these young persons, the middle school and junior high school were created to ease the transition from elementary school to high school. Movement between schools is a major stressor for most adolescents. Not only does the work get harder, but other changes in the young person's life make it more difficult to concentrate on school. Young adolescents going into middle school must deal with new faces, move from class to class, and be more anonymous than they were previously—all at a time when they're feeling more self-conscious anyway!

Most children adapt well to this transition, though some experience such problems as lowered academic motivation, lowered self-esteem, and an increase in behavioral acting out. Young adolescent girls, in particular, may experience significant drops in self-esteem due to the significant number of life changes faced by female teens.[20] Of great concern is the additional finding that for a number of these teens, recovery in self-esteem is not likely. One reason why there may be negative changes in the transition to middle school is that the adolescent is confronted with many stresses at the same time. As teachers get more demanding, the teen's grades may go down, and she appears distracted and unmotivated when she feels out of place, tries to cope with pubertal changes, and struggles to keep up with her peers. Parents may also have a hard time acknowledging that their child is not a baby anymore, and may overprotect the teenager or subtly reinforce immature behaviors. As a result of these stresses, some teens get into downward spirals of lowered grades, drops in self-esteem, negative expectations about their abilities, and avoidance of or resistance to schoolwork.

For most adolescents, high school is not only an academic experience but also an opportunity to practice social skills. Teenagers learn new material and skills that prepare them for college or careers; they also participate in clubs and sports activities and spend a considerable amount of time socializing with friends.

Although the high school dropout rate has declined over the past twenty years, it remains a serious problem, particularly for minority groups, such as Latino Americans and Native Americans. A teen's dropping out of high school is usually a result of a combination of factors, such as poor reading skills, early school failures, low motivation, impoverished background, and disrupted family situation—if we therapists hope to keep the teen in school, we need to address these factors as early as possible. We also should always assess the nature and quality of the young person's school environment in order to keep an adolescent in school and maximize his or her experience.

High school is the time that many adolescents begin to think consciously about making career decisions. Many factors enter into the equation, including abilities, personality, parents' support, and chance. Although some studies show little difference in vocational choice between high school males and females, gender is still a major factor in career decisions: females are still socialized into traditional roles, and counselors often steer young women into gender-typed careers. For many minority adolescents, career choices are limited by the absence of role models, lack of economic resources, and racial discrimination. Mental health professionals need to assist all young people to make career choices based on their individual abilities and help them believe they have the power to influence their lives.

## EMOTIONAL DEVELOPMENT

Many parents with whom I've consulted over the years worry about moods, because the wild fluctuations in their child's emotions often occur daily and unpredictably. As therapists we too experience the highs and lows of our young clients and need to evaluate the extent and depth of the teen's emotions in relation to developmental norms. Much of our sense of what is normal or excessive comes with experience; books can only hint at how much anxiety in the adolescent is too much, or when normal angst crosses the line and becomes clinical depression for a specific teen.

I write this section in the hope of alerting you to what emotions are part of normal development and how these might look in teens who are at risk for developing more serious disorders. Many emotional displays are related to the physical and school issues discussed earlier in the chapter or to the identity issues discussed later. Because emotional displays are often connected to problems in these other areas, we need to look beyond the emotions themselves, evaluate the seriousness of the situation, and explore the antecedent and resultant behaviors related to the feelings.

## Anxiety

It's not unusual for adolescents to feel self-conscious, shy, and modest. They become anxious about what they wear, how they walk and talk, and whether other kids are talking about them. I remember Sam, a thirteen-year-old client, who always sounded different on the telephone than he did when he was with me in my office. Unsure of who was calling and wanting to make sure he sounded mature, Sam would always answer the phone with a very deep voice, in case the caller was a schoolmate. Natasha, a fourteen-year-old ninth grader, would often tell me that she was sure the kids were whispering about her, especially the boys. She felt anxious and hypervigilant, particularly if she had to walk by a group of these boys on her way home from school.

Are these behaviors normal? In and of themselves, yes! As I've said, adolescents are by definition self-centered, and they imagine that others are as concerned about their behaviors as they are. So because they are feeling strange about their body and feelings, they assume that everyone else sees them as strange, and they agonize about being normal. Certain types and degrees of anxiety, then, aren't worrisome, and we need to understand the feelings as a natural part of development. What's critical is for us to understand what precipitates the anxiety and what coping mechanisms the adolescent uses to deal with it.

## Depression

Depression is common to adolescents, as they struggle with new feelings and experiences and are faced with making decisions that might affect the rest of their lives. Research suggests that 2.5 to 4 percent of children in the general population suffer from clinical depression;[21] the figure is as high as 61 percent in a psychiatric population.[22] Adolescents who are depressed show social isolation, decreased school performance, increased family conflict, and increased risk of suicide.[23]

It's often difficult for teens or their parents to tell the difference between normal blues and true clinical depression.

---

Kayesha was a sixteen-year-old African American girl. When her mother called me, she was frightened. Kayesha seemed "upset" lately, according to mom. She reported that Kayesha was often down on herself, never happy with her appearance; she often fought with her parents. What precipitated the phone call to me was Kayesha screaming at her parents, "I wish I was dead," in the middle of an argument.

I agreed to meet Kayesha, who was a bit resistant at first but quickly warmed up once she realized I was not an agent of her parents. She was bright and verbal, had many friends, played competitive soccer, and had plans to attend a state college in a year and a half and major in communications. She acknowledged being unhappy with her appearance at times and feeling some sadness that she wasn't as close to her parents as she used to be. After some additional assessment, I told Kayesha's mother in a family session that I thought the young woman was going through some normal adolescent growing pains and invited the whole family to come in for a few sessions to help them communicate more effectively and to reorganize their family as Kayesha prepared to leave for college.

---

Was Kayesha's mom right to call me? Absolutely! Parents should always take seriously their child's sadness, and so should we. In terms of treatment planning, we must then assess whether the sadness reflects normal development, a primary clinical depression, or a depression secondary to other psychological issues (such as low self-esteem or family problems).

## IDENTITY DEVELOPMENT

The critical task of adolescence is the development of a unique identity, a sense of self. Although answering the question, "Who am I?" is a lifelong journey, the struggle to come up with an answer peaks in adolescence as teenagers make decisions about how they will live the rest of their lives. The physical and intellectual changes discussed earlier prepare a young person to seek an answer to this question, as adolescents are constantly confronted with life choices: What options do I have? What risks will I take? What values will I live by?

Erik Erikson concluded that adolescents must use the skills they've learned in childhood to make decisions about how they will fit into society.[24] According to Erikson, resolving the crisis of identity versus identity confusion becomes the central task of adolescence. It is at this time that an adolescent must determine a sense of self; if they do not develop a sense of who they are and where they belong, a sense of identity confusion results, and the teenager may feel aimless and insecure.

A certain amount of identity confusion is normal and may help explain some teenage behavior. Katie becomes obsessed about her clothes, her hair, and her makeup. Nick makes impulsive decisions, guided more by the peers he happens to be with on a particular day than by any internal sense of what is right. Jesse gets an earring and starts listening only to punk rock music. Trish wonders if she should go to college or work for a year or two. Juanita struggles to reconcile her desires to be like her friends with following the norms of her culture.

All these young people are struggling with the challenge of choosing what to believe in. Their parents have presented them with values and a lifestyle, and now the teens must decide for themselves in which directions to go and to which values they will commit. One of the tasks of therapy with adolescents is to help them make such commitments in ways that don't compromise their safety and that allow for resolution of the identity conflict within a reasonable time frame.

For adolescents of the majority culture, who have access to many resources, identity development is complex enough, but it is particularly complicated for minority teens. Such young people must struggle with integrating the values of their own culture with those of the dominant culture; they also must strive to understand what it means for them to be different than their peers of the majority culture in many ways.[25]

In the past twenty years, researchers have expanded on Erikson's theory. James Marcia examined the roles of crisis and commitment in identity development.[26] He defined *crisis* as a period of conscious decision making, and *commitment* as a personal investment in an ideology. He then identified four *identity statuses* according to the presence or absence of crisis and commitment:

1. *Identity achievement:* an adolescent has struggled with her options and has made a strong commitment to a life plan (commitment after extensive exploration).

2. *Foreclosure:* the young person has committed to a plan based on other people's (for example, parents') choices rather than

going through a crisis period himself (commitment without exploration).

3. *Identity diffusion:* a teenager may be considering options but is not agonizing over them and has yet to make commitments (no commitment and no exploration).

4. *Moratorium:* the adolescent is actively struggling with a decision and has not made a commitment (exploration but no commitment).

Marcia's subsequent research on gender differences led him to find that men in moratorium were similar to men in the identity achievement category; for men, achieving identity involved an extensive period of exploration. However, women who resembled men who had achieved identity were in foreclosure! That is, women had achieved identity by making a commitment but without having gone through a personal crisis and period of exploration. Women thus seemed to make premature identity decisions based more on others' choices for them than on appraising their own goals and choices. Marcia concluded that for women, foreclosure seemed to be adaptive, because women were pressured by society to carry on social values from one generation to the next rather than discover their own unique identities.

Other researchers have questioned whether this foreclosure is really adaptive for females at the turn of the century. Notably, Carol Gilligan, through interviews with girls in several age groups, has concluded that females do in fact achieve identity more through cooperation than competition.[27] However, their accepting societal notions of how they should be (similar to the foreclosure status) may be at the expense of girls' self-confidence and self-esteem. Women often solve identity dilemmas by keeping their opinions to themselves so as to stay connected to others, and they lose self-confidence in the process.[28]

---

Lindsay, a high school senior, was referred to her counselor after a teacher found her crying in the bathroom. She tearfully talked about how confused she was about all the decisions she had to make, about friends, boyfriends, and her future. She felt overwhelmed by competing demands for her time and about having to decide what she was going to do once school was over. Lindsay was everyone's friend and confidant, but now that her peers were about to go their separate ways, she felt lost. Not surprisingly, Lindsay wanted the counselor to tell her what to do, and had a very difficult time answering the question, "What do *you* want?"

---

In our work with adolescents we need to stay alert to the possibility that lowered self-esteem in teenage girls may be a result of their denying their true feelings in an attempt to resolve the identity crisis.

## Sexual Identity Development

Adolescents' sexuality strongly influences their developing identity. Teenagers experiment with all kinds of sexual activity, experience a variety of sexual and romantic feelings, and seek intimacy in relationships. Conflicts about sexual feelings or behaviors sometimes bring adolescents into therapy, and we need to keep in mind that experimenting with certain sexual behaviors does not necessarily lead to a sexual identity.

For example, about 15 percent of boys and 10 percent of girls have had a homosexual experience during adolescence, although only 3 percent of teenage boys and 2 percent of girls have ongoing homosexual relationships.[29] Despite a young person's fears that a same-sex fantasy or experience "makes them a homosexual," sexual orientation is determined by a complex interaction of biological and environmental factors. Helping adolescents explore their sexual orientation and values and arrive at their own conclusions may become a focus of treatment.

## Renegotiating Family Relationships

Establishing identity in adolescence typically involves separating from family and forming intimate relationships with peers. Although popular beliefs suggest that this process is tumultuous and highly con-flictual, research evidence indicates that adolescent rebellion is not the norm.[30] In fact, most adolescents feel close to their parents, have similar values on major issues, and appreciate their parents' approval. Significant conflict is reported to occur in only 15 to 25 percent of all families and may have been present before the children became adolescents.[31]

This is not to say that some conflict doesn't occur in most fam-ilies, only that the intensity may be more of a myth than a reality. For example, even though teenagers are more independent, parents still attempt to teach them to conform to societal rules and family values. It is often just this independence that frightens parents, because they may view their child as rejecting all of the lessons they've taught him or her over the years. As a result, arguments about personal appearance, schoolwork, and chores are common.

In the process of establishing their identity, adolescents want to be able to decide things for themselves. Believing that they are capa-ble of knowing what's best for themselves, teenagers will argue with authority figures about dating, curfew, and house rules. They feel ready to take risks, believing in their own invulnerability. I remem-ber arguing with my own parents when, on a stormy day in New York City, I received my driver's license in the mail and wanted to take my friends to a party despite never having driven alone.

The presence of mild family conflict, then, is a normal develop-mental process. Most disagreements between the teenager and his or her parents are resolved in a way that everyone can live with and that both allows the parents to maintain their integrity and supports the adolescent in developing a clear identity. Becoming independent doesn't mean completely severing ties with parents; as a matter of fact, adolescents who consider themselves autonomous typically view their parents as close role models and often turn to them for advice.[32] What is necessary is a gradual renegotiation of the parent-child relationship to one of greater mutuality. Conflict allows teens and their parents to restructure their relationship; when such conflicts are severe and not resolved easily, counseling may be important to help the adolescent avoid developing more serious problems.

## Relationships with Peers

As teens and their parents renegotiate family relationships, adolescents form new relationships with peers. Although the common belief that teenagers reject their parents and come to depend totally on their peers is a myth, it is true that adolescents do turn more to their peers as a reference group for their identity development. Other teens become a source of support and understanding, because they are going through the same struggles. The peer group also becomes a place to experiment with new behaviors and to form intimate relationships. Harry Stack Sullivan discussed the importance in adolescence of what he termed *chumship*. Such chumships give teenagers needed support as they begin to pull away from their parents and establish their own identity, and many therapists suggest that we should attempt to facilitate such chumship relationships between our adolescent client and his peers.[33]

Communication with peers also changes; because adolescents are better able than children to express their thoughts and feelings and to understand others' points of view, they tend to share more with their friends than do younger children. Studies show that teenagers spend more than half their waking hours with peers and are happiest when with friends—no wonder they're often on the phone with friends within minutes of having seen them at school or at a party!

The impact of so-called peer pressure in the life of an adolescent cannot be underestimated, but research evidence reveals some interesting details. For example, peer influence seems strongest in the eighth and ninth grades, just at the time the struggle for independence is at a peak;[34] susceptibility to peer influence decreases as the teenager gets older.[35] Also, peer influence is strongest around everyday social issues, such as dress, school, and drugs and alcohol, and can be positive as well as negative.

Other research indicates, however, that adolescents choose as friends those who think and act as they do to begin with. Teenagers who smoke or drink seek each other out, as do adolescents who are aggressive, show high or low school achievement, are antisocial, or show anxiety or depression.[36] Thus when parents in a first session attribute their child's behavior to peer pressure, it's important for us to keep in mind that peers are just part of the picture and that the parents still have a major impact on the adolescent's behavior.

---

This chapter has provided an overview of normal adolescent development. I've tried to illustrate that adolescence is a tumultuous time, full of changes in the physical, intellectual, emotional, and identity realms. Because adolescence is such a turbulent time, it is often difficult to know what is and isn't normal, and many teens, parents, and even therapists feel pretty hopeless about the adolescent at times.

Yet the bulk of the research presents a very positive view of adolescence. Most young people are happy with themselves and their lives, get along well with parents and peers, feel confident about their abilities, and manage developmental stresses quite well. They do not show problems related to physical, cognitive, or emotional development, and they are progressively answering the question, "Who am I?" About 20 percent of teenagers, however, do show significant problems and would benefit from psychological treatment.[37] In the next chapter, I'll describe typical problems related to adolescent development and discuss how teenagers present to therapists.

# 2

# Presenting Problems

In Chapter One we covered the processes and tasks teenagers face in the normal course of development. For most young people, this process proceeds like driving an automobile over cobblestone streets: there are some bumps, maybe some slight delays, but adolescents get to their destination intact and ready to handle the demands of adulthood. For some, however, the engine sputters badly, and the car won't move; for others, the auto has to back up because it missed critical turns. Like an auto mechanic, a therapist must then diagnose the problem and offer anything from a minor tune-up to a major overhaul.

There are numerous ways in which adolescents and their families present their concerns to therapists. Sometimes parents and teenagers present their concerns directly and explicitly, such as "Johnny won't go to sleep until he's checked the locks on all the doors and windows," or "Susie won't eat anything but yogurt." At other times, referral sources or the adolescent himself will describe a behavior in vague terms, such as "William doesn't seem happy," or "Betsy is hanging out with the wrong crowd."

Part of our job in the early stages of the counseling is to make sense of these behaviors, both in terms of how they fit into an overall picture of the teen as well as how they relate to a diagnosis. Our adolescent client may be exhibiting behaviors that are manifestations of a yet unexplored underlying problem, and it may take several sessions for us to get a complete picture. Unless the present-ing problem is a crisis situation that needs immediate attention, I would advise you to take your time doing this assessment, and to concentrate during the first session on establishing a working rela-tionship with the teenager.

Although I have divided presenting problems into categories, remember that with our adolescent clients, a particular behavior may reflect one of several problems, and we need to understand the etiology of the behavior as we develop treatment plans.

Some problems, such as schizophrenia, have a biological com-ponent to their etiology; others are primarily acute reactions to a trauma, such as violence. Most presenting problems in adolescents, though, can be seen as functions of distorted or arrested develop-ment. The biological, cognitive, and social changes that are part of normal adolescent development all put stress on teenagers and their families and demand healthy adaptation. Questions young people have about such things as sexuality and identity leave them vul-nerable to various influences, some not so positive, and put them at risk for adjustment difficulties.

As discussed in Chapter One, we must view all behaviors in ado-lescents against developmental norms if we are to make sound diag-nostic judgments. Counselors unfamiliar with such norms might assess a teenager's behavior as more pathological than it is; for example, they might assume that a teenager's growing need for pri-vacy was an indicator of depression. Uninformed practitioners might also underestimate the seriousness of the young person's behavior; for example, they might attribute experimentation with drugs as merely a "rite of passage."

We must also assess behaviors in terms of degree and context; what seems normal to some extent and in some circumstances may be problematic in others. For example, some self-consciousness and withdrawal are to be expected; if the teenager withdraws from most of his friends, however, there may be a problem. Everyone has some idiosyncrasies, but these may not be pathological unless they bring about psychological pain or discomfort, or interfere with the quality of the young person's life.

Knowledge of developmental psychopathology is also invaluable to effective therapeutic work with adolescents, because the symptoms of many disorders vary with age.[1] For example, for children diagnosed with attention deficit hyperactivity disorder (ADHD), such symptoms as impulsivity and inattentiveness are much more likely to be evident during adolescence than is hyperactivity, which is more common in childhood.[2] Other researchers have noted similar age differences for other disorders, such as conduct problems and anxiety. Regarding depression, for example, adolescent girls tend to exhibit symptoms of withdrawal, whereas younger girls are unlikely to exhibit this symptom.[3]

During adolescence there are increases in the rates of depression, bipolar affective disorders, attempted and completed suicide, and schizophrenia.[4] Agoraphobia and social phobias become more common than in childhood, whereas enuresis and encopresis occur less frequently during the teen years. Antisocial activity goes up in frequency of activity but not in the number of individuals involved. Without thorough knowledge of developmental psychopathology, "the therapist may be prone to apply inappropriate treatments or to be overly concerned about the presence of certain symptoms."[5]

Knowledge of development derived only from Caucasian, middle-class American norms is not enough, however. In determining where behaviors lie on the normal-abnormal continuum, we need to take into account not only the client's individual development and his or her family life cycle but also the influences of other systems, such as school, religion, economics, and the adolescent's culture. For example, not making eye contact does not necessarily indicate low self-esteem; feeling suspicious of others may not suggest paranoia.

---

I once worked with a seventeen-year-old college freshman from Indonesia. Her presenting problem was that a male in some of her classes was interested in her—he would sit next to her, offer to carry her books, and invite her for coffee after class. She told me she did not want to date this young man and wanted him to leave her alone. I presented several alternatives and asked if she'd considered them; she responded, "Oh no, I couldn't do that" to even the mildest of them. I began to wonder if this young woman had terribly low self-esteem or severe assertiveness problems, until I asked her what she would do if this problem occurred in her home country. She quickly answered, "I would tell my father; he would take care of it." I invited a colleague of mine who had visited Indonesia extensively into our next session so that we could work out a plan acceptable to my young client within her cultural mandates.

---

In this chapter, I'll talk about disturbances in the developmental processes described in Chapter One. My discussion is based on the assumption that in an attempt to master developmental tasks, some adolescents or their families (or both) underreact, overreact, or react inappropriately to normal stresses and demands. Underreaction can consist of not providing essential information to the young person, overlooking early signs of distress, or not setting reasonable and timely limits for the child. Overreaction often means losing perspective on what's normal, engaging in power struggles, or not giving the young person needed space and autonomy. Inappropriate reactions involve solutions to stresses that may relieve the immediate anxiety but that are destructive patterns in the long run; for example, a teen may isolate himself if he feels a little self-conscious or diet unhealthfully when she gains a little weight.

## EMOTIONAL DISTURBANCES

In this section I've included problems of adolescents that are characterized by troubling emotions. Sometimes teenagers express these emotions directly, such as in anxiety or depressive disorders; other times, the primary symptoms are behavioral, such as self-mutilation, but may be considered emotionally based.

## Anxiety and Fears

Anxiety disorders affect people of all ages, and are characterized by subjective distress (anxiety or fear) and behavioral disturbances. Adolescents may be affected by anxiety disorders that are more characteristic of children. For example, teens may seem overanxious: they worry about trivial things, are unable to relax, and have an excessive need for reassurance. They may also suffer from separation anxiety, evidenced by extreme difficulty in being apart from an attachment figure—such young adolescents often refuse to attend school as a result. Other anxious teens avoid social interactions with unfamiliar people and may appear shy and unassertive.

Adolescents may also be diagnosed with anxiety disorders typical of adults.[6] For example, they may suffer from simple fears and phobias, social phobia, panic disorder, and obsessive-compulsive disorder.[7]

---

Callie was always known as "hyper." She talked fast, shook her leg constantly, and had a hard time staying on task. Over a period of time, her grades began to drop, her sleep became restless, she suffered from shortness of breath, and she had trouble keeping food down.

---

Chad's self-consciousness started in elementary school, where he was considerably smaller than his classmates. By middle school, the size gap had widened, and Chad was picked on by peers and responded with some minor aggressive behavior. By high school, Chad had begun avoiding others and had developed a true social phobia, including occasional panic attacks in class and staying away from school events where there were crowds.

---

George had been a good student in elementary school. Despite his parents' insistence that they didn't pressure him, George developed perfectionistic standards for himself by the time he entered junior high school. Although striving to be perfect is not unusual in adolescence, George's standards were extreme, and the smallest error sent him into tirades about how stupid he was. He often stayed up very late, redoing projects until they were perfect. He also developed other compulsive traits, such as laying out the clothes he was going to wear the next day in a particular order and eating his food in a ritualized manner.

---

Clearly the symptoms Callie, Chad, and George were experiencing were beyond normal limits, and these young people needed therapeutic attention. In an initial session, we need to understand these teens' behaviors as anxiety based and to plan treatment accordingly.

There are two key factors I've found helpful in differentiating "normal" adolescent anxiety from that which necessitates intervention. The first factor is the extent to which the anxiety dominates the teenager's life: How pervasive is it (as in a generalized anxiety disorder)? How strongly does the teen experience it, such that he or she has direct symptoms, such as stomach pains or breathing problems? With what normal activities of a teenager's life does it interfere, such as socializing?

The second factor regards whether the anxiety leads to dysfunctional or highly annoying behavior. In the "dysfunctional" category would go such behaviors as phobias, obsessive-compulsive rituals, substance abuse, eating or sleep problems, and the like. We must remember that adolescents engaging in these kinds of behaviors might not define the behaviors as dysfunctional, so our clinical judgment comes into play as to whether or not the teen's behaviors are normal or problematic. In the "annoying" category, often defined by the youth or his or her family, would go avoidance of previously enjoyable activities (such as sporting events or parties); habits that create individual or interpersonal stress (for example, foot tapping or constant need for reassurance); or ineffectiveness in certain activities (such as completing assignments).

In the initial sessions with the adolescent and her family, we need to ask specific questions about the presenting problem so we can assess how persuasive and intense the symptoms are, as well as whether the behaviors themselves are dysfunctional or highly annoying. Our assessment and diagnosis skills are vital to drawing these conclusions, but I hope you'll find the factors I've presented in this section useful guidelines in beginning the diagnostic process.

As they do in childhood, fears in adolescence reflect developments in physical maturation, in cognitive abilities, in relationships, and in identity. Fears of pain and bodily injury, along with fear of animals, decline in adolescence, but some irrational fears persist, such as fear of the dark, of mice and snakes, and of storms and noise.[8] Because adolescence brings with it an increase in the cognitive ability to project into the future, teenagers may experience an increase in fears about war and peace, and personal worries about being able to cope with future problems. Sexual fears and concerns about work and finances also emerge in the teen years.[9]

Many fears that present initially in adolescence concern the teenager's developing identity and self-consciousness. One example is fear of failure or personal inadequacy, often expressed in school phobias. Adolescent girls may begin to experience fear of success, thought to be related to sex-role expectations that females shouldn't outdo their male counterparts. Teenage girls in particular may express strong concerns about being popular, and all adolescents are fearful of looking foolish.

## Depression and Suicide

It's always important for us to take seriously a young person's sadness or withdrawal. Yet it is also essential not to jump to conclusions before doing a thorough assessment. Several researchers have attempted to define the experience of depression in adolescence, reporting such symptoms as social isolation, alcohol and marijuana use, frequent crying, daydreaming, and thoughts of suicide.[10]

Depression in adolescence is often masked by other disorders, such as school phobias, anorexia, and some conduct disorders.[11] Many depressed adolescents complain of boredom, inability to concentrate, and apathy, or show irritability, weight loss, concentration problems, and somatic symptoms.[12] The first occurrence of bipolar disorder may occur in adolescence, and significant depressive symptoms may precede the initial manic episode.[13]

So what do we look for in making a diagnosis of depression? Many symptoms of teen depression are classic: withdrawal, apathy, loss of pleasure in most activities, tiredness, sleep or eating problems, and feelings of helplessness and hopelessness. Teens also express their depression in ways that are unique to adolescence— school problems, delinquency, substance abuse, sulking and irritability, angry outbursts, unstable behavior, and problems with peers.

We should always compare the teen's symptoms to his or her usual behavior as well, because what we're looking for in making a diagnosis of depression are changes in normal activities. When changes in adolescents' behavior are dramatic or extreme, we should always consider the adolescent at risk for suicide; suicide continues to be a leading cause of death among teenagers, second only to accidents.[14] Studies have provided the following data on teen suicides: ten suicide threats are made by adolescents for each teenager who actually attempts, and nine attempts are made by adolescents for each teenager who actually completes suicide.[15] The research further shows that the completed act was preceded by a four- to six-week period of depressive symptoms, physical complaints, and behavioral changes. Direct or indirect suicidal intent, as well as breakdowns in communication with friends and parents, were common. Some of these adolescents had attempted suicide previously, and many drank large amounts of alcohol a few hours before the act.[16] In addition, a major confrontation with a meaningful person generally occurred on the adolescents' last day, and many made a desperate attempt to contact a friend before killing themselves.

When adolescents present with depressive symptoms, we must spend part of the initial session assessing risk factors. Look for feelings of worthlessness, feeling under pressure to perform, and use of alcohol and drugs. Suicidal youth tend to be impulsive, to have low frustration tolerance, and to be socially isolated. They may have suffered a recent loss or disappointment and may give away prized possessions. Access to lethal instruments, such as guns, is problematic. Another factor to consider is sexual orientation; approximately 30 percent of teen suicides are gay and, as a result of societal attitudes, typically feel alone and unsupported. We need to bring up the issue of suicide with the depressed adolescent and not be afraid that doing so will put ideas into his or her head.

## Obsessive-Compulsive Disorders

Obsessive-compulsive disorder (OCD) can start at any time from preschool age to adulthood. It often goes undiagnosed, however, because people with OCD may be secretive about their symptoms or they or their families lack insight about the disorder. In adolescents, OCD may go unrecognized because some of the behaviors look like exaggerations of normal childhood rituals, such as bedtime prayers or checking to see if the doors and windows are locked. At other times, the stresses of adolescence may increase certain fears the adolescent already has, leading to compulsive behaviors that dissipate over time. But when the obsessive or compulsive symptoms persist and interfere with functioning, they need attention.

The thoughts and actions that constitute OCD in adolescents are similar to those for adults. The teenager may worry excessively about contamination, losing control, or having to keep things in order. He or she may engage in compulsive acts, such as checking things repeatedly or counting objects over and over. Keep in mind, of course, that all teens are self-conscious, and they worry about things they've said or done that they think have made them look bad. It's also normal for adolescents to appear pretty compulsive about their hair or clothing. Yet these behaviors usually don't persist or cause much distress, as we would expect in OCD.

Whereas depression often accompanies OCD in adults, it is less common in adolescents with the disorder. However, OCD in teenagers can cause or worsen disruptive behaviors, exaggerate preexisting learning disorders, cause problems with attention and concentration, or interfere with learning at school. OCD behaviors also may elicit negative comments from family members or from school personnel, so we have to do some work with these systems as well as with the teen. For example, we may need to discuss with the adolescent's family and teacher the fact that his problems at home and in school are a result of his depression, not part of a willful act.

## Self-Mutilation

Self-mutilation is a pathological behavior that is most prevalent in female adolescents. Self-mutilation has been linked to such adolescent developmental issues as individuation, overwhelming emotional changes, identity formation, and emerging sexuality.[17]

Some of the most relevant symptoms that should alert you to look for possible self-mutilation are the teenager's difficulty verbalizing emotions and needs, her difficulties controlling emotions, and severe struggles with establishing an identity.

## Schizophrenia

Adolescents who are diagnosed schizophrenic may show some of the same fears or anxieties already noted, but their symptoms are usually more chronic or severe. As is typical of those persons diagnosed with other psychotic disorders, schizophrenic teens may evidence a distorted sense of reality as well as visual-motor deficits. Interpersonally, they present to us as withdrawn, emotionally distant, and detached from the therapeutic process.

# DISRUPTIVE BEHAVIOR DISORDERS

This group of disorders includes attention deficit hyperactivity disorder (ADHD), conduct disorder, and oppositional-defiant disorder (ODD). Adolescents with disorders in this category are typically aggressive, impulsive, and often destructive. They show high levels of activity, resist discipline, and exhibit lapses in concentration.[18]

## Attention Deficit Hyperactivity Disorder

An adolescent with ADHD is often initially referred by his or her teacher, who notices the teen's high activity level, impulsive behavior, inability to sustain attention in class, and problems following instructions. Because of these traits, such individuals are easily distracted, have a difficult time paying attention to the teacher, and may fail to complete assignments, particularly those that have little intrinsic appeal.[19] They may present as fidgety and restless, disruptive in class or in a therapeutic interview, and as demanding much of the teacher's or counselor's attention. Parents also will talk about the teen as careless, unable to sustain a task, and as "hyper" much of the time.

A hallmark of the disorder is impulsivity, or a failure to stop and think before responding to a task.[20] During adolescence, the primary symptoms of inattention and impulsivity are typically less severe than might have been seen in childhood, yet they are still significantly different from normal.[21] A thorough assessment for ADHD is critical in adolescence, as this disorder may explain other presenting problems, such as poor school performance, difficult peer relationships, or conduct disorders.

## Oppositional-Defiant Disorder

Young adolescents who have a history of ADHD sometimes develop more serious disturbances of conduct. Their high activity level and low frustration tolerance often create interpersonal problems with teachers, peers, and family members.

Jacob was a thirteen-year-old who had been diagnosed with ADHD at age eight by his pediatrician. He was prescribed Ritalin, which seemed to help, though after five years Jacob complained that it "zoned him out," and he took the medicine only sporadically. Jacob's teacher related to his parents that the boy often didn't turn in assignments, behaved like the class clown, and frequently talked back to her. At the first family session, the parents agreed that Jacob behaved this way at home as well; he would often argue with them for no apparent reason and had a teenage version of temper tantrums: shouting, name-calling, and slamming doors. He also refused to comply with his parents' requests and sometimes did just the opposite of what they asked. The depth and breadth of these outbursts were beyond what I considered as normal adolescent emotional displays—I diagnosed Jacob with ODD.

## Conduct Disorder

Symptoms of ADHD and ODD, such as hyperactivity, noncompliance, and aggression, may also be present in conduct-disordered youth.[22] Early adolescents may begin a pattern of poor school performance, truancy, aggressive behaviors toward peers, school suspensions, and running away. Once their oppositional behavior involves serious rule violations, we need to consider the diagnosis of conduct disorder.

These young people have moved beyond a defiant stance toward authority to one of repeated acts of aggression, truancy, shoplifting, and the like. Aggressive behaviors may include violence against persons or property (for example, vandalism, fire setting); nonaggressive conduct problems often involve breaking rules (such as abusing substances, running away).

It is important to understand that the characteristics often associated with conduct disorders may also occur in the context of other symptoms. For example, in a sample of hospitalized adolescents who had been diagnosed with conduct disorders, 56 percent had at some time been diagnosed as psychotic, 61 percent as learning disabled, and 45 percent as neurotic or adjustment-disordered.[23] Depression may also be present, although we can miss noticing this because the more provocative behavior distracts us.[24] Successful diagnosis and treatment of conduct disorders in adolescents is vital, as many studies have shown that adults diagnosed as antisocial were showing conduct-disordered behavior at earlier ages.[25]

## Substance Abuse

Although the rates for adolescent use of most chemical substances has decreased, abuse is still a major problem and is comorbid with other problems such as depression and delinquency. Working with teens who are abusing substances poses major challenges for us as therapists, because such factors as biological addiction, personal reinforcers (such as anxiety reduction), and social pressure (modeling, peers) make treatment difficult. Alcohol, tobacco, and drug use are so common among adolescents that some teens often feel weird and estranged if they *don't* use. Several teenage clients have mentioned to me that they felt ostracized by certain groups of peers, and had actually considered smoking or drinking as a way to gain acceptance in this group.

Substance abuse may become apparent to parents or others through overt signs, such as evidence of drugs or drug paraphernalia. Typically, though, substance abuse is manifested through other behaviors; from a psychological perspective, these behaviors reflect a delay in normal maturation.[26] Substance abusers tend to have low self-esteem, and may deal with some of the stresses of adolescence by turning to drugs rather than by learning more mature, effective coping mechanisms.

Presenting problems may include a drop in academic performance, physical changes (for example, red eyes, runny nose, fatigue, coughing, or wheezing), changes in eating or sleeping habits, or lack of interest in personal appearance. Socially, substance-abusing teens may show increasing signs of withdrawal and isolation, or a change in friends; relationships with family members often deteriorate as well. These adolescents may also show problems with impulse control and delaying gratification, so they appear more rebellious, aggressive, and hostile.

I've always found substance-abusing teenagers to be among the most resistant participants in therapy; they are often dragged to session by a parent or mandated by probation as a result of a delinquent act. These teens have a hard time connecting their behavior problems with the substance abuse and may have not yet experienced a history of negative consequences due to their drug use. Thus their denial is stronger than it is in most adolescents; adolescents deny problems, although substance-abusing teens deny problems even stronger and you need to be careful not to confront the substance abuse too directly in the initial sessions. Rather than ask directly whether or not a teen is using drugs, I always ask what kinds of substances he or she uses and how often.

## BODY IMAGE ISSUES

Because teenagers want to be like their peers, anything that sets them apart can be very upsetting. Young teens can be pretty cruel toward peers who are different in some way, so kids who mature early or late can suffer from anxiety, depression, loneliness, or low self-esteem.

---

Andy was fourteen years old and a freshman in high school, but he was barely five feet tall and very skinny. A pretty gregarious kid most of his life, Andy started isolating himself around age thirteen, and he occasionally got referred by his teachers for acting like the class clown. He was often viciously teased by his classmates, who told him that he belonged back in middle school. Desperate to be accepted, Andy tried to joke around and make others laugh, behaviors that had worked when he was younger. But now his actions just evoked further rejection and teasing from his peers, leading to further withdrawal and loneliness.

---

Suzanne was eleven when she started to develop, and by the time she was twelve and a seventh grader, she was bigger than her peers and had full breasts. Once a good athlete, she was now awkward on the playing field and slower than the other girls on her team. Suzanne tried wearing loose-fitting clothing and started a pattern of dieting in hope that she could get her body back to the way it used to be.

---

Because it's not unusual for adolescents to seem preoccupied with their looks and to think of themselves as too tall or too short, too skinny or too fat, or unattractive in some other way, we need to be able to separate normal self-consciousness from excessive worry. Both boys and girls during the teenage years worry about their physical appearance, but females tend to be unhappier about the way they look than males of the same age. Because of this, adolescent girls are more prone to depression and self-esteem problems that can carry over to adulthood. When taking a developmental history, then, you should gather information on both the actual pubertal changes in the teen as well as on the reactions of the young person and of significant others to these changes.

## Eating Disorders

The preoccupation with one's looks often affects the teenager's eating habits, and 15 percent of adolescents suffer from obesity. Weight problems are a major health concern, because obese teenagers tend to become obese adults. During the teen years, though, the major issue becomes one of social isolation: being overweight invites rejection by peers. People also often look down on the obese adolescent because they believe he or she has no willpower; we need always to keep in mind that a person's becoming overweight is not simply a matter of willpower—it is a result of a combination of factors, some biological, some environmental. We can provide essential support to young people trying to lose weight so that other, more serious problems, such as anorexia or bulimia, don't occur.

Because societal pressure on teenage girls to remain thin are intense, adolescents sometimes develop a poor body image if they don't look like the models in teen magazines. Poor body image will often lead teenagers to attempt to control their weight in unhealthy ways, such as yo-yo dieting or self-starvation. Anorexia and bulimia have thus become all too common among adolescents. Recent studies have suggested that as many as two-thirds of high school girls and 15 percent of boys are preoccupied with weight and dieting and that up to 1 percent of teenage girls suffer from anorexia. Prevalence rates increase to 5 to 7 percent of adolescents who experience vocational pressure to stay thin, such as ballet dancers.[27] Prevalence rates for bulimia are estimated to be 4 to 5 percent in white high school and college samples, although as much as 8 to 20 percent of the female population engage in episodes of bingeing and purging.[28]

Because adolescents often keep anorexia and bulimia secret from others, they may not reveal their eating disorder in an initial session. In fact, even when confronted with evidence, these teens may deny the extent of the problem, as they are often terrified of giving up this coping strategy. Instead, such teenagers may present in acute distress related to the eating disorder but want the therapist to give them a quick solution to the distress, not to the eating problem itself. Often, of course, girls who severely restrict their food intake look incredibly thin, so the disorder is apparent to others as well as to the therapist. Bulimics, in contrast, do not look abnormally thin, so they have an easier time keeping their eating habits hidden from others.

---

Early in my career, I worked with Amy, a seventeen-year-old college freshman. Amy presented with some homesickness and experienced some sadness, occasional crying for no apparent reason, and some difficulty studying. I assumed the changes in her eating behavior were due to depression, so I didn't pursue the topic until, at the third session, she brought me an article on bulimia she had found in the newspaper, which she said I might find interesting.

---

Because of this encounter, and knowing that the majority of teenage girls are weight conscious, I now routinely ask adolescent female clients about their eating habits and body image. If a teenage client looks very thin, it's important that we raise the issue of her eating habits in the first session and ask if she's had a good physical checkup recently. These young women may not readily talk about these patterns directly, though, so you would be wise to stay alert to the signs of these disorders, described in the next paragraphs.

Anorexics typically have very distorted body images, so they won't acknowledge your concerns that they look thin; in fact, they'll feel successful if you point out that they are thin! Often they present as high achieving and perfectionistic, obsessed with rituals (about food preparation, for example) and doing well in school—though they may also be withdrawn and depressed and feel out of control of their emotions. They are often described by their parents as model children, and they usually don't show much of a rebellious attitude or behavior.[29]

Bulimics also present as high achieving and perfectionistic; they constantly worry about how they look to others and are fearful of losing control. Bulimics often suffer from physical symptoms such as tooth decay, skin problems, stomach irritation, and loss of hair; they often engage in rigorous exercise routines or use laxatives or diuretics. The binge eating may be precipitated by an emotional crisis, and after an eating episode bulimics may present to a therapist with depression, shame, and extreme self-contempt.[30]

# IDENTITY CONCERNS

In the search to define their identity, adolescents experiment with new behaviors in relationship to their peers and parents. They typically move from close friendships only with same-sex peers to romantic relationships with other teens, and in this way establish a sexual identity. They also begin to pull away from their parents and establish their own set of values. In the following section, I'll discuss some of the problems teens face in establishing sexual and personal identity.

I'll also discuss two other issues related to identity—school problems and trauma. These are included in this section because the stresses associated with these issues potentially shake the adolescent's sense of self, and can lead to additional stesses for the teenager.

Most of the issues presented in this section can thus be understood as identity concerns, even though the presenting symptoms seem more related to physical or emotional issues. With some older adolescents, the identity issues are straightforward—they present with explicit identity issues, such as "Who am I?" "Where do I fit in?" "I don't feel close to anyone," or "I feel like I keep picking the wrong person to date." Along with these kinds of questions and feelings, such teens typically present with self-confidence, depressed affect, or hopeless cognitions. Some teens might tell counselors that they don't know what courses to take or what to major in, or whether to go to college or get a job after graduation.

## Sexual Behavior, Teenage Pregnancy, and Parenthood

Some adolescents engage in promiscuous sexual behavior in their quest to establish a sexual identity. They become sexually active to keep up with peers, to prove their maturity, and to establish romantic relationships. Teens often engage in sex as a substitute for real intimacy, but doing so may actually have the opposite effect of what the young person is looking for—that is, the sex leads them to feel less connected, worse about themselves, and more confused about relationships.

Ask adolescents if they are sexually active and what their experiences have meant to them. Exploration of identity issues early in treatment may help clarify why the adolescent engages in sexual behavior and prevent teens from putting themselves at risk for STDs and pregnancy.

Some pregnant teens will seek counseling to discuss options related to their pregnancy. Given their sense of invulnerability, they may be shocked that they're pregnant, frightened and naive about all the ramifications of pregnancy, and scared to tell their friends and parents. They also must make decisions about school, employment, marriage, and finances. Helping the adolescent figure out these practical issues is a central focus for treatment.

Clinicians working with pregnant teens also need to address other psychological and emotional issues. Pregnant and parenting adolescents often present with depression, social isolation, and poor interpersonal skills.[31] They may also feel alienated from their families and show a preference for risk-taking behaviors. Although you may need to deal with the practical issues first, you should also assess these other symptoms early in treatment.

## Sexual Identity

In the process of adolescent development, teenagers must come to grips with their sexual identity. For those teenagers who identify themselves as lesbian, gay, or bisexual (LGB), acknowledging and accepting their sexual identity often becomes a formidable task. Considering that approximately one out of every four families in the United States has a gay or lesbian family member, it is imperative that we be knowledgeable about the therapeutic issues that arise in the LGB adolescent's establishing of his or her sexual identity.[32]

LGB adolescents may present in therapy with issues related to one or both of the developmental tasks facing these young people: what Savin-Williams terms *self-labeling* and *first disclosure*.[33] "Self-labeling is a series of internal processes by which individuals become aware, recognize, and then define their sexuality as lesbian, gay, or bisexual."[34] First disclosure involves the individual's revealing his or her desires or experiences, and usually occurs to a best friend. Some adolescents recognize their homoerotic desires but won't reveal them to anyone; others disclose to friends through their behavior but deny these desires to themselves. Counseling includes helping young persons resolve both tasks: honestly labeling their same-sex attraction and deciding when and to whom they can disclose.

Initially, LGB youths struggling with their sexual identity may present as isolated and lonely, particularly if they have felt that they had to hide their orientation.[35] They may withdraw from peers, and present with depressive symptoms, such as low motivation, eating and sleep problems, and negative cognitions. As Savin-Williams notes, these teens may adopt a "self-deprecating or negative identity . . . at a time when most other youths are gradually building self-esteem and establishing a positive identity."[36]

Several authors have noted that a common adolescent response to the fear of disclosure is to try extra hard to pass as heterosexual, for example, by making jokes about homosexuals or becoming sexually promiscuous.[37] However, this behavior usually leads to feelings of awkwardness and depression. When LGB teens are harassed by others, they may show generalized anxiety, school problems, phobias, substance abuse, prostitution, self-destructive behaviors, depression, and suicidality; LGB youths are two to three times more likely to commit suicide than heterosexual youth.[38]

If LGB teens are referred for psychotherapy, it is more likely that the referral will be for one of these other disorders; these young people will typically not bring up the topic of sexual orientation in therapy and may even lie to you if asked directly in an initial session. However, Savin-Williams does suggest that a practitioner can help young persons develop trust in the process if the therapist uses nonheterosexist language (such as *partner* instead of *boyfriend* or *girlfriend*) with adolescent clients.[39]

## Relationship Problems

Considering that a hallmark of adolescent development is the process of renegotiating family relationships and developing peer relationships, it is not surprising that adolescents sometimes present to counselors with relationship problems. These issues run the gamut from the angst of first love to more serious issues, such as violence or intense familial power struggles. For an example of the former, recall the client I mentioned in Chapter One who, in the waiting room, met me with a cry of "I hope you're good, because I don't think even God could help me with this problem!"

Parents often bring their adolescent to see me, complaining of the teen's bad attitude or disruptive behavior or gross habits. They and the teen detail significant arguments and communication problems, and ongoing power struggles. Adolescents in difficult family relationships will present with a range of reactions, from withdrawal to substance abuse to delinquency; such behaviors often reflect a sense of frustration and hopelessness. Although it's important for us to have some individual sessions with the young person who describes family conflicts, I've always found it critical in these circumstances to include the family in treatment so that rules and roles can be renegotiated in a productive manner.

## Academic and School Problems

Some of the issues adolescents present to counselors center around school. Although poor grades and academic failures may be the symptoms presented, we always need to differentiate problems that result from cognitive or learning deficits from those that result from emotional problems or identity struggles.

---

Jamie was a thirteen-year-old eighth grader who had done well in elementary school but was doing progressively worse and worse in middle school. According to her mom, a single parent, Jamie typically would say that she had finished her homework or didn't have any, and then would spend most of the evening alone in her room listening to music. Jamie's advisory teacher had noted many instances of homework not being turned in, however, and that Jamie was developing a pattern of truancy. In Jamie's case, her mom had gone back to work recently, and Jamie would return home from school to an empty house. Having been somewhat of a teacher's pet in elementary school, Jamie was feeling particularly alone in middle school, where she found that her personality didn't count for much if she couldn't do the work. In addition, her two best friends were much more interested in boys than she was, so they often left her out of their plans.

When Jamie showed up for her initial session, she presented with symptoms typical of teens having academic difficulties. She was bored with school and unmotivated, and felt that the teachers picked on her and were unfair. She said that she often felt distracted and had a hard time concentrating, and sometimes felt really dumb. "I know the stuff," she explained, "but when it comes time to answer questions in class or do my homework, it's like it's not in my head anymore."

---

Some school problems reflect a cognitive deficit, such as a learning disability or an attentional disorder. The earlier these problems are identified, the better, as drops in school performance can quickly lead to a vicious cycle in which low grades lead to a drop in self-esteem and self-confidence, which in turn lead to further drops in school performance. Although most learning disorders or ADHD will become apparent before adolescence, it is possible that a teen has figured out how to compensate for these difficulties or that the school did not pick up on the problem. Thus a previously unrecognized learning disability may be contributing to the young person's school problem. Referrals to medical doctors, educational psychologists, or both for comprehensive learning evaluations are often necessary.

Because academic problems may also result from difficulties in making the transition from elementary school, we should assess the teen not only from an academic viewpoint but also from a more psychological perspective. Does he feel overwhelmed? What is her level of self-confidence? Is he feeling comfortable and connected to peers? Does she have support at home for schoolwork and her changing needs? Sometimes these teens will look depressed, as they experience more and more helplessness and fall further behind. Other teens will react to school problems by giving up and turning to delinquent activities such as truancy, substance abuse, or gang behavior.

As described in Chapter One, the high school years present the adolescent with new intellectual and personal challenges.

---

When he turned sixteen, James was told by his mom that he had to work to help support the family. James was the oldest of four children from three different fathers, none of whom were around any longer. Needless to say, James's grades dropped dramatically; having no role model for academic success, James was losing interest in school and considering dropping out. When his teacher heard what he was considering, she referred him for counseling. James was very conflicted: he wanted to stay in school but also felt loyal to his family; so if he did poorly in school and flunked out, the decision would have been made for him. The counselor discussed realistic options with James, such as working part-time, and brought his mother and older siblings in for a family session.

---

As they must with young adolescents, therapists working with high school–age teenagers need to assess both their cognitive and intellectual potential as well as the psychological and family issues that are affecting these young people. Identifying the source of school difficulties should enable us to plan treatment accordingly;

that is, we might recommend family therapy, job training, career planning, tutoring, substance abuse treatment, and so on, depending on the needs of the individual teen.

## Victims of Trauma

Teenagers may be referred for psychological help because they have been the victim of a traumatic event, such as peer suicide, death of a family member, being a witness to a crime, or being physically assaulted or raped. These teens are in a crisis, which is sometimes experienced immediately and other times may hit them later on. Particularly for adolescents, who, as part of their normal develop-ment, view themselves as indestructible, such traumatic occurrences shake their self-confidence and ability to cope, as they struggle with trying to make sense out of these senseless acts.

In general, teens in crisis may present as lost and in shock, as feeling overwhelmed with sadness and worry. They may be hyper-vigilant, as if fearful that danger will somehow attack them again, and they may develop obsessive thoughts or rituals to control their anxiety. Some will have difficulty concentrating, become restless and irritable, and have trouble sleeping and eating. Young victims may get angry and express this anger through self-destructive be-haviors or aggressive acts toward others. Some will present with sur-vivor guilt, wondering whether there was anything they could have done to prevent the act and why they survived when others didn't.

## Victims of Assault or Rape

The overwhelming number of sexual assault victims are female, but we need to remember that adolescent males are also subject to acts of sexual violence. Keep in mind that when male teens present with some of the following symptoms, we should ask them about being assaulted.

Physical assault and rape are acts of violence, and they leave the victim feeling powerless. Particularly if the attack was by an acquaintance or a date, the woman may blame herself for being naive or foolish, for not stopping the attack, for having trusted the perpetrator in the first place, or even for causing the assault—it's not at all unusual for victims to present to clinicians as guilt ridden and overly self-deprecating.

Oftentimes, adolescents who have been assaulted or raped are in denial; they want to put the experience in the past and just get on with their lives. In such situations they present to a counselor as emotionally flat and not wanting to talk about their experience or feelings. Once the therapist helps the young woman get past this resistance to talk about the assault, what typically emerges is a trauma syndrome that includes fear of being alone, fear of specific people or of men in general, and fear of further assault.

Survivors of assault may tell us that they are worried about what their friends and family will think if they find out, reflecting doubt that they can ever trust anyone again. The young woman may experience physical problems, such as stomachaches, headaches, and other signs of stress. Her feelings often include anxiety, guilt, embarrassment, anger, and helplessness. It's only after a counselor helps the teenager deal with these fears and emotions that a victim can truly be a survivor and regain a sense of control over her life.

## Posttraumatic Stress Disorder

We may diagnostically classify victims of assault or rape as having a posttraumatic stress disorder (PTSD), which may be acute or delayed. PTSD may be caused by any number of events that are generally considered traumatic, ranging from natural disasters (such as tornadoes or earthquakes) to those created by humans (accidents, divorce, abuse, and the like). The recent killings on high school campuses are a prime example of how vulnerable adolescents are to acute trauma.

Symptoms may depend, in part, on the age of the adolescent. Younger teens may be more adversely affected by traumas that separate them from caregivers, whereas older adolescents may be more sensitive to events related to their identity development, such as peer suicides. At any age, however, teenagers are susceptible to reexperiencing the traumatic event through intrusive recollections or dreams in which the event seems to reoccur.[40]

As discussed earlier, teens exposed to a trauma may initially appear numb. They may lose interest in activities or people they previously enjoyed, thus slowing down or bringing to a halt activities necessary to identity formation. Some become hyperalert, have difficulty sleeping, experience somatic symptoms, and can't concentrate. As a result of these factors, they may fail to finish assignments and have a hard time focusing in class, causing their school performance to drop. Others may act out in destructive ways, including being aggressive toward others and toward themselves; suicidal ideation may also increase. It's not unusual for older teens to express a sense of helplessness to a counselor, reflecting a belief that they're not in control of environmental events.

---

Marta was fifteen when her boyfriend was killed in front of her in a drive-by shooting that appeared to be gang related. Not only did Marta become hypervigilant out of a realistic fear of being killed herself, but she kept reliving the event in her mind, wondering if she somehow could have saved her boyfriend. She couldn't keep food down, had very restless sleep, and increasingly withdrew from her family and friends. After voicing such concerns as "What's it all about?" "If they want to kill you, they will," and "It's my fault he's dead," Marta took an overdose of her mother's sleeping pills and was brought to the emergency room and then transferred to the psych unit.

In the initial session in the hospital, she appeared detached and with flat affect, and repeated to the therapist some of the same pessimistic thoughts. One of the major goals of the treatment was to help Marta feel empowered to control her life again.

---

What I've tried to show in the preceding two chapters is that the adolescent phase of life span development can be a turbulent time for both the teenager and his or her family. The developmental needs of the adolescent are substantially different from those of a child; rapid physical growth sparked by puberty, changes in cognitive abilities, the task of integrating conflictual emotions, new academic challenges, and the renegotiating family and peer relationships all demand healthy adaptation.

When teens and their parents handle these changes appropriately, young persons are able to gain a clear, positive self-image that enables them to move into young adulthood. When they do not handle these demands well, however, adolescents struggle to clarify their identity. They may not learn how to deal with their impulses in self-enhancing ways. Their fears may prevent them from experimentation, or they may make ill-informed decisions. They may experience considerable distress or develop symptomatic behaviors that cause concern for others. It is these teens who will show up at our doorstep.

# 3

# Preparing for the First Session

Now that we've reviewed normal adolescent development and how teenagers might present themselves to us in therapy, we can think about getting ready to meet the young person and his or her family. You can enhance your effectiveness with adolescents by preparing in advance for the first session. Although each teen and each story is unique, I've found certain attitudes and procedures helpful with all my adolescent clients.

## UNIQUE ASPECTS OF COUNSELING WITH ADOLESCENTS

Unless they are mandated by the court, most adults enter psychotherapy voluntarily. Certainly, some adults will insist that the only reason they called you was to appease another person, such as a spouse, but ultimately the adult made the decision to begin treatment. This is not typically the case with adolescents.

Some teenagers, particularly older ones, may initiate therapy, but generally we see adolescents because someone else decided the young person needed help. Parents, school personnel, friends, or sometimes the police or the courts recognize that a problem exists; the adolescent may not agree and is often "forced" to start counseling by these others. In fact, some adolescents really don't understand why they've even been brought to my office! A colleague of mine said it nicely: "When it comes to counseling with adolescents, the parents are the consumers . . . the teenagers are merely visitors."

## Forming an Alliance

During an initial session, then, you should not expect or press teenagers to admit they have a problem; doing so will likely result in their distrusting the process, because they will conclude that you are just like every other adult who doesn't understand them and just wants to bug them. Instead, think of the first session as an opportunity to establish a working relationship with the young person and to motivate the adolescent to take a look at his or her life. One example of a way to engage the client in the process is to frame the situation as the adults' problem and challenge the teen to help you understand why the adult has the problem. You can negotiate some goals with your young clients, even if initially the goal is simply to get the adults off their backs!

---

I once worked with a thirteen-year-old who was brought in by his parents because they had found out he was smoking marijuana. On confronting him about this, they learned that he sometimes snuck out in the middle of the night to smoke with friends and occasionally skipped school and spent the day getting high. The adolescent made it very clear right up front that he had no intention of stopping his marijuana use, so it was useless for his parents to waste their money on therapy.

After sending his parents out of the room, I made it clear to him that I was not at all interested in whether he smoked or not—what I was interested in was helping him find out why his parents were so worried about him, and how he could help them with *their* worry so they wouldn't give him such a hard time about the marijuana.

## Clarifying Misperceptions

Even if an adolescent is aware that a problem exists, he or she might not choose therapy as the way to solve it. Adults voluntarily entering treatment usually have at least a vague understanding of how talking about a problem will help, but adolescents don't often have this understanding and may already feel "talked to" enough by the adults in their lives. They may also have stereotyped views of psychotherapy based on what they've seen on TV or in the movies; some expect us to label, criticize, or scold them in some way, and others expect us to play with them, hug them, or take them out to eat. In preparing for the first session, we need to anticipate this lack of knowledge and these misperceptions about treatment and be ready to educate the teenager a bit about the process.

---

When I first met Will in juvenile hall, he was already defensive about the "shrink" coming to see him. When we got to the counseling office, which was actually the nurse's office, Will immediately looked around for a one-way mirror and asked where the couch was. He was also sure I was there to find out if he was crazy and that I would report everything he said to his mother and probation officer. I assured Will that although I had to report danger or abuse, I would keep the details of our sessions confidential unless he gave me permission to release information. I also told him that I was asked to see him because others (for example, his probation officer) were worried about him but that what we talked about was up to him and me. I further explained that I had no desire to tell him how to run his life, but if there was anything I could help him figure out, including how to get others to cut him some slack, I would try my best to do so. Although suspicious and somewhat disbelieving of my assurances about confidentiality, Will seemed less anxious after I clarified my role, for whom I was working, and what counseling would involve.

## Having Some Props

Although in many respects they are more adultlike than childlike, many teenagers don't have the verbal skills with which to express themselves. Relying only on talk therapy with these clients would prove to be frustrating for both these adolescents and us. Although we shouldn't talk down to teens or offer them play equipment used with younger children, our having age-appropriate games and creative materials, or being willing to go for a walk or shoot baskets, can go a long way in establishing rapport.

I always have baseball cards, CDs, art supplies, magic tricks, and board games available and in full view in my office; in a hospital or detention center, I often suggest going outside. Keep in mind that a primary goal of the initial session is building a therapeutic relationship; you'll have much more time to actually counsel the adolescent, but your effectiveness is directly related to the strength of the connection you make in this first session. The materials or activities mentioned above often help me achieve some common ground with my young clients in the initial session.

# WHOM TO INVITE
# TO THE FIRST SESSION

The question of whom to invite is directly related to your theoretical orientation as well as to pragmatics. More analytically oriented therapists may want to get a detailed developmental history of the client before beginning treatment. Thus they often see the parents first for a couple of sessions, particularly when working with younger teens who might not be able to provide necessary information. These therapists sometimes see older adolescents alone for a few sessions so that a positive transference might develop and teenagers can begin to view the therapist as working for *them*, not their parents.

In contrast, more process- and systems-oriented counselors often prefer to obtain information as they go along so that they can see information in a meaningful context. This approach doesn't imply that these therapists ignore the past, only that a detailed history isn't critical before beginning treatment. Thus it is unlikely that these practitioners will invite the parents to be seen first; even if they see the adolescent individually at first, they bring significant others into the sessions soon afterwards.

## Involving the Family

My own style is more in line with systems thinking; I believe that, except in a crisis situation, the symptoms displayed by the adolescent usually reflect a family problem, and that in order to understand the problem it is essential to view the adolescent in his or her interpersonal context, that is, the family. This approach does not preclude having subsequent sessions with the teen apart from the family; actually, I have found individual sessions intermingled with family sessions to be extremely helpful in my work with teens. Whenever possible, however, I always insist that the entire family, including extended family who live in the household, be present in the initial session.

Having everyone present is very useful from a pragmatic viewpoint. Because a teen may not believe he has a problem or may have a radically different perspective on what the problem is, he may present as clueless as to why he needs to talk with us. Having a family member initially define the problem in front of the teen allows the adolescent to disagree or refocus the issue.

Not only is involving the family dictated by my understanding of most teenage problems and by practical considerations, but I've found the support of the family critical to the success of my work with minors, because I may give the teen homework or ask family members to make some changes. In Chapter Five I describe how I conduct an initial session when the family is present; even when I do see the family together first, there is of course always a time at which I do a "first session" with adolescents themselves. This might be a part of the session in which the family is present, or it may be a more lengthy individual interview later on. My most favored approach is to see the entire family for the first session, the adolescent alone for the second, the parent(s) alone for the third, and the entire family for the fourth.

I then spend subsequent sessions primarily with the teenager, and invite specific family members to join the session as the need arises. So even though I see most problems of adolescence as emerging from the interactions within the young person's family, I think it's respectful to the teenager and to the process of his or her individuation from the family to see the teenager alone much of the time.

## Working with the Adolescent When the Family Isn't Available

Therapists who are strongly systems-oriented must deal with the pragmatics of treatment situations that sometimes make it impossible to have the family together in the initial session. In school settings, for example, counselors may have little or no access to the family for the duration of therapy; the only contact may be through a written authorization for treatment brought home by the student and returned to the counselor. Likewise, in a detention center or juvenile hall, a therapist may have only minimal telephone contact with the family. I've had to learn to engage the adolescent, then, without much background information or the luxury of viewing the teenager in the context of his or her family.

In these cases, the referring person (for example, the probation officer or teacher) becomes the main source of information about the teen (aside from the teen herself) and can give us only a snapshot of the young person's life without the benefit of history or of having seen the adolescent in a variety of contexts. It is very helpful to get this referring person's sense of the teenager, if not before the first session then soon afterwards. Important information to obtain from the referring person includes not only the specific identified problem ("She's fighting with her peers," "He defaced the school with spray paint") but also this person's perception of the teenager's moods, coping mechanisms, and interpersonal relationships in general.

When meeting with adolescents in these circumstances, I still give them a chance to respond to others' concerns (as described in Chapter Five). I still ask teenagers about their own perceptions of various aspects of their lives, but I tend to focus more on their lives in the context of the referral. Specifically, if the referral comes from the parents, and I meet with the family in an initial session, I spend more time talking about family and interpersonal issues. If I see the teen in juvenile hall, I have the adolescent talk more about what it's like to be locked up and unable to see friends and family. If my initial contact is in a school setting, I talk with the young person about classes, peers at school, teachers, and so on.

At other times, legal restraints prevent us from meeting with the young person and his or her family. For example, we may be called in to meet with a teenage victim of sexual or physical abuse; if the perpetrator is a parent or guardian, that person may be forbidden to be in contact with the minor. This scenario, too, challenges us to begin treatment with little to no input from family members. In Chapter Five I'll discuss engaging the adolescent without having met the family in the first session.

## LEGAL ISSUES

In working with minors, you always need to be aware of legal issues in your state. In some states children as young as twelve may consent to treatment without parental permission under specific circumstances. In California, for example, a minor twelve years old or older may give his or her consent to treatment for a drug- or alcohol-related problem without parental consent, although therapists need to document in their notes why, in their opinion, it was not appropriate to contact the parent. Consent of parents or guardian is also not required in a crisis or if, in the opinion of the clinician, the minor (age twelve or older) is mature enough to participate intelligently in the treatment and would present a danger of serious harm to himself or herself without counseling, or has been the alleged victim of incest or child abuse.

In the event that you have a "reasonable suspicion" of physical or sexual abuse, you must make a report to the local authorities and child protective services. The minor may then be taken out of the home and put in a protected environment, and the county may assume parental rights. If this occurs, whoever has these rights must authorize continued treatment of the teenager.

## Consent and Assent to Treatment

Despite these exceptions, most state statutes require parental consent in the treatment of minors. Even when the young person seeks counseling himself or herself, it is very risky for you to see the teenager without parental consent. Thus therapists working with adolescents should always have parents or legal guardians sign a Consent to Treat Minors form at the first session. As well, you should always attempt to obtain the "assent" of the teenager as early in the treatment as possible—doing so shows respect for the teen as an emerging adult despite the fact that he or she doesn't have a legal right to refuse treatment.

## Single-Parent Consent to Treatment

What if the adolescent is brought to treatment by a single parent? It may be *legal* for us to treat the minor with only one parent's consent, but it may not be best therapeutically to do so. If parents share joint legal custody, regardless of where the child lives, typically they are ordered by the court to share in decisions concerning the child's health care; thus the other parent, on hearing that her teen is in therapy, may ask the court to order termination of the treatment. In the meantime, she can make life miserable for the adolescent and sabotage the counseling. I always make a sincere attempt to get the consent of both parents before beginning treatment, and if the custodial parent refuses to allow me to contact the other parent, I typically will refuse to work with the minor.

When the initial call to me comes from a single parent I ask the parent who sought treatment for the teenager whether she has joint legal custody with the minor's other parent. If she does, I tell her that this usually means that both parents need to make decisions concerning the adolescent's health care. I also remind her that sometimes a child's problems have something to do with his parents and that I may need to call on both parents at some point in the treatment. I conclude by stating that for these two reasons, I make it a practice always to have both parents consent to treatment. If she refuses to allow the other parent to be contacted, I then tell her that short of a court order allowing her to make a unilateral decision, I'll have to refer the child to another therapist. The only exceptions I'll make are in a crisis, such as when a teen is suicidal, or if the other parent is nowhere to be found; in the latter case, I'll document in my notes that I failed in my attempts to contact the other parent.

## Informed Consent

In order to secure valid parental consent, we need to inform the parents of the nature, purpose, and potential risks involved in treatment. In addition to providing their written Consent to Treat Minors, all family members should sign an Informed Consent agreement. Included in this agreement should be (1) a complete explanation of the treatment and its risks, discomforts, and benefits; (2) a description of other possible treatment alternatives; (3) an offer to discuss the procedures or answer any questions; and (4) information that the client is free to withdraw consent at any time and discontinue treatment.

Teenagers should also be informed of these aspects in language they can understand, although they need to know that their parents have the legal right to secure or terminate treatment. For example, I tell the adolescent that counseling is an opportunity for her to talk to me about her life and any problems or concerns she has and that I'll try my best to help her figure out the problem and come up with some solutions. I add that because I understand many problems to be the result of family relationships, I plan to bring her parents in for some sessions but will always discuss with her what will happen in the family sessions prior to the meeting itself.

I offer to answer any questions the minor client might have about what we're doing or why I'm asking certain questions, and tell him that if I believe another therapist or another form of treatment might be more effective, I'll discuss this with him. I then discuss confidentiality (described in the next section) and the client's legal rights and those of his parents.

## Confidentiality and Access to Records

In our work with minors, confidentiality is always a critical issue, and we're faced with conflicting demands. On one side are adolescents, who are often obsessively concerned with privacy; fearful that any secrets told to their therapist will get back to their parents, they may withhold information and approach the process with intense distrust. On the other side are their parents, who are sometimes so distrustful of the teen that they *do* want the counselor to reveal everything said by their child. How should we handle this situation?

My Informed Consent form, the content of which I reiterate during the initial session, states that I will not reveal to the parents what is told to me by the adolescent, except for instances in which I am required to do so by law (such as in cases of child abuse or a threat of violence). I indicate that I will, if requested, give to the parents my general impressions of how the teen is doing, but preferably in family sessions with the teen present. Similarly, I detail that I will not relay information from the parents to the adolescent— this also must be given, if possible, in a family session.

I tell both adolescents and their parents that in order for me to do my best work, I must be the one who decides what information the adults should receive. I assure everyone that if in my judgment the young person is putting himself or herself or others in danger, I may choose to break confidentiality, but that in general it is not useful to the treatment if the parents press either me or the teenager for information.

As already mentioned, I also prefer not to be the conduit of information from parent to minor, or vice versa. If long-lasting change is to take place, family members must learn ways to communicate effectively with each other, without using a third party. I assure the teenager that if there is something I think the parents need to know, I will always discuss it with him or her first and try to work out a way for the teen to present it in a family meeting. When this approach is not possible, as in situations in which I cannot have family meetings, we talk about ways the teen can effectively present the information to the family.

I also tell family members that I will not bring up with the adolescent something the parents ask me to without revealing the source and without giving the minor a choice as to whether or not she wants to discuss it. I think it's terribly deceitful and can backfire dramatically if I receive information from the parents and then mysteriously and seemingly out of the blue ask the young person if she has gotten any school referrals, or gotten into fights, or had a bulimic episode the previous week.

## Access to School Records

Whereas parents do not have direct access to a private clinician's records without a court order, they typically do have access to school records. Counselors in schools thus cannot make the same promises of confidentiality as an independent practitioner or clinic staff member can. However, some school counselors keep separate records of treatment, which do not become part of school records and are viewed as similar to a private clinician's records.

It is also important to remember that a noncustodial parent or guardian may have the same access to a minor's educational records as the custodial parent, so we need to take this into account when writing notes and discussing confidentiality. It's essential, therefore, that we inform the custodial parent that the other parent has the right to discuss the minor's treatment with us and to view whatever is in the teen's school file. I make certain, though, that when I write case notes, I indicate the source of my notes so that if they are subpoenaed, it will be clear to the court whether the adolescent, the custodial parent, or another person relayed certain information to me.

# THERAPIST SELF-DISCLOSURE

Adolescents often ask personal questions of us or comment on how we look, how our offices are decorated, or why we would want to do such work. Much of this is a natural curiosity; remember, teenagers are trying to make sense out of the world and wondering where they fit in. They may have heard or read about psychotherapy but probably have never met a therapist or been to a clinician's office. Because we don't want to be overly formal and want to encourage engagement during the initial session, anticipating questions and preparing ways to answer can be very helpful to the process.

## Deciding When and How to Disclose

As when you are working with adults, your decisions about disclosing yourself to teenagers should be guided by your judgment as to what they are really asking, how much information they can tolerate, whether or not they will benefit from the disclosure, and how the question makes you feel. Even when you do choose to disclose, you must always be concerned about the potential impact on the minor.

Teenagers will often ask me questions about what a psychologist is, how long I've been doing this work, and whether or not I have children of my own. I always answer these inquiries briefly but directly. They may go on to ask if I've had problems similar to theirs: Have I ever been depressed? Had a homosexual experience? Smoked pot? With these kinds of questions I'm more likely to avoid answering directly; I instead respond that, like them, "I've had some difficult times in my life," or "I've done some things that left me anxious or confused," or "I didn't always follow the rules myself." Often this is enough to establish a connection. If pushed for details, I might share a memory or two of cheating on a test or falling asleep in class or leaving a restaurant without paying or even making someone cry—but I quickly move back to "Tell me more about what happened with you."

If the teen still pressures you for private details of your life, one way to handle this is to acknowledge the adolescent client's desire to get to know you, and to remind him that the focus of your discussion needs to stay on him. I might say, "I can appreciate your wanting to know about my life. Right now, I'm not comfortable sharing that information, though I might at some point in the future. My job is to see if I can help *you* figure out your own answers to these questions, so why don't you tell me more about what happened to you."

They may also ask about my children—did they ever get into trouble? What did I do as their parent? I typically acknowledge that my kids, like all young people, had some rough times and that I'm certain I didn't always handle the situation in the best possible way. I then may ask my teenage clients what they think a parent should do, and stay alert to signs of anger or disappointment in the way their parents handled them.

## Facilitating Rapport Through Disclosure

I've often had wonderful discussions with my teenage clients about objects in my office—my baseball autographs, drawings done by other kids, books on my shelves, even a little owl sculpture once given to me by a client. Sharing what's important to me often opens up a dialogue about what's important to them. When I see adolescents in another setting, such as a school or juvenile hall, I sometimes make common cause by telling them what they would see in my office and asking them what their room at home looks like, or by sharing some recent experience I've had and wondering if they have ever done anything like it.

One of the things adolescents, like other clients, often do is ask a lot of questions as a way to shift the focus away from them or to create discomfort in us. A female intern of mine reported that in her work in juvenile probation, male clients would sometimes ask her personal, sexually oriented questions. Although refusing to answer directly seemed evasive to her, she was also uncomfortable about revealing details about her life. Through supervision she learned the difference between a question asked by a teenager to establish a common bond and one meant to evoke a reaction. She gained an awareness of how critical it was to set appropriate limits with these minors and to maintain her boundaries, particularly because these teens may not have good boundaries themselves. She learned that even though it might seem evasive, refusing to divulge information about certain aspects of her personal life was good modeling for the minor. My intern began telling provocative minors, "I don't mind answering certain questions about my life, but let's get it straight right now that talking about my sex life is out of bounds." She also got a little creative at times, saying, "If I want to talk about my sex life, I'll go see my own therapist. Right now, let's talk about you."

## CULTURALLY RESPONSIVE COUNSELING

Many of our adolescent clients come from cultural backgrounds different from our own; it is thus imperative for us to be aware of our own biases, stereotypes, and worldview as well as to be knowledgeable about the specific culture of the client. Minority adolescents may not understand the counseling process, and our therapeutic approach may be inconsistent with their experience. For example, minority teens may be uncomfortable talking about personal issues with someone who is not part of their family, or may not be used to talking about feelings. We must see the teenager's values and behaviors in a cultural context and be careful about misunderstanding adolescents by comparing them to the norms of our own cultural group.

In preparing to meet with a teenager from a different culture or background, you should already have done your homework, in terms of both developing your self-awareness and expanding your knowledge base. You will want to have some information on culture-specific customs and practices, because when working with minority adolescents you may have to modify some of the traditional ways you establish rapport. For example, self-disclosure, eye contact, use of first names, and slang expressions may have different meanings to teens from different cultural backgrounds. It may be important for you to explain to the adolescent why you are asking personal questions, so as not to seem overly intrusive.

You can also facilitate engagement with adolescents from different cultures if you have a thorough knowledge of racial and ethnic identity development, and by involving them in discussions of salient cultural themes. For example, a recent article by April Jackson-Gilfort and Howard Liddle detailed how "discussions of anger, alienation, and journey from boyhood to manhood" were helpful in establishing working relationships with African American youth.[1]

In working with adolescents from culturally diverse backgrounds, you would be wise to take an idiographic approach; that is, you should focus your counseling on the experience and context of the specific teenager and be prepared to use treatment modalities that fit the client. Thus, even though it is important for you to understand the cultural background of the young person, you should not treat all adolescents from a particular culture the same way. In addition, you might find that an informed, creative use of extended family and other indigenous support systems goes a long way in helping the teen who comes from a culturally diverse background.

When I'm about to meet with an adolescent or a family from a background different than my own, I take a hard look at my own assumptions and try to keep in mind culturally relevant information.

Sharing my understanding (or lack thereof) with the client and not trying to move him or her in a culturally inappropriate direction have helped me gain credibility with many young people.

---

When we work with adolescents, we can never predict with much accuracy how a young person will present in the initial session. Nevertheless, I've found that my knowledge of developmental norms and of the issues adolescents typically present, and preparing in advance for the specific clients and situations I'm about to encounter, can help me meet the teenager with a sense of confidence and focus. Let's look now at conducting the first session itself. In Chapter Four I'll share some attitudes and behaviors I find helpful in my work with teenagers, and in Chapter Five I'll describe the actual process of the initial session.

# 4

# The First Session

The first session is absolutely critical to the success of the treatment of adolescents, because what happens in this meeting sets the tone and establishes patterns for future sessions. Several researchers have noted the negative expectations and assumptions adolescents bring into counseling, the difficulty of reversing a negative therapeutic alliance, and the importance of a positive therapeutic relationship to outcome.[1] Clearly, knowing how to conduct the initial session effectively is essential.

It should be obvious by now that counseling with adolescents is an extremely challenging task, so challenging that many clinicians actively avoid it. Many of the same attitudes and behaviors that have gotten the teenager in trouble are brought into treatment, creating anxiety and consternation in even the most experienced therapist. As we would expect from a developmental standpoint, adolescents in therapy are often uncooperative with the therapist, and they make it clear that they view the whole idea of therapy with disdain. For anyone who has worked with teenage clients, the following scenario will be familiar.

---

Enrique, sixteen years old, was arrested for vandalizing his school and was referred by the probation department as part of a juvenile diversion program. His counselor, an intern I supervised, met Enrique at the youth's new alternative school, where individual counseling and anger management classes were a central part of the program.

The intern described Enrique to me as "totally resistant." He went on to say that the young man sat with his arms folded, wouldn't look at him, and responded to his questions with eye rolls or "I don't know." The intern attempted to use techniques he had learned in his classes, such as asking open-ended questions, making empathic statements, or bringing up safer topics, but to no avail. Needless to say, the intern was not looking forward to the next session—and I'll bet the client wasn't either!

---

Enrique had to return for another session; therapy was part of his probation so he had little choice as to whether or not he attended sessions. With many teenagers, though, just getting them to come back for the second session is a major challenge. Obviously, therapy cannot succeed if it doesn't even take place! Most experienced clinicians would agree with Liddle that the most common challenges for therapists working with adolescents are "How do you get teenagers to attend, participate, and remain in therapy?"[2] In this chapter and the next, I'll share my experiences of trying to answer these questions.

In this chapter we'll review strategies for engaging the adolescent in the treatment. I'll present several attitudes and behaviors I've found very useful in establishing working relationships with my teenage clients. In Chapter Five we will look at the process of the first session itself. I'll present a step-by-step guide to conducting the initial session, and to dealing with resistances that might emerge in the teen or his family. Although these two chapters are certainly not intended to be a cookbook for success, I'm hopeful that you will find some of these ideas helpful in your work with teens.

Engaging adolescents is a difficult process, as they are often distrustful, oppositional, and self-protective. Their experience with authority figures may have been negative and conflictual, they're tired of adults trying to control them, they're naturally self-conscious, and they don't understand why they have to talk to a "stupid shrink" anyway! How can we behave with adolescents in order to overcome these obstacles and enhance the therapeutic relationship?

# HELPFUL ATTITUDES

Doing effective work with adolescents involves more than learning a cookbook of techniques. As with most counseling, the relationship between the therapist and the teenager is what's going to make the difference in the young person's life. Sure, there are things we can do or not do to enhance the therapeutic relationship, and I'll talk about these later on in this chapter. But there are also attitudes toward teenagers that are helpful, if not essential, to effective work with them.

## Liking Teenagers

Needless to say, it's helpful if you like teenagers and like working with them. When my graduate students tell me they really don't like kids and find adolescents particularly irritating, I advise them to concentrate their fieldwork elsewhere. Until these clinicians can find some joy in being around teens, their young clients won't feel safe enough to open up to them.

I've spent many years in nonclinical interactions with teenagers as well as with adolescent clients. Having raised three children of my own, coached their sports teams, lived with them through the angst of their first loves, cried with them over their pain and disappointments, I've come to appreciate how difficult it is to be a teenager in today's world. I loved watching their attempts to be so grown up and adult, followed by their childlike tears when they were sick and wanted some comfort. I admired their resiliency in the face of anguish, and their ability to capture life just the way it really is. Whenever I got distracted, their brutal honesty brought me back to dealing with the important issues in life, such as family and relationships.

## Liking Your Client

Similarly, it's very helpful if you can find something likable in your specific client. Adolescents are particularly sensitive to signs of rejection and may resist any attempts by their therapist to establish a relationship if they sense that the clinician doesn't like them. Let's remember that some of these young people have elicited dislike and scorn from adults already, so they expect us to respond to them in the same way. And some of them do act so cruelly or rudely that it's hard to really like them.

Certainly, I've met some teens over the years who, try as I must, I just didn't like. Although I came to like a few of these young people over the course of our time together, there were others for whom I never could develop a liking, and I never got very far in treatment with them.

If you find yourself in this situation, try putting aside the therapy work for a while and go back to a focus on engaging the adolescent in ways I'll describe in this chapter. Let yourself be playful and intrigued by the young person instead of seeing him as a client. And you should always consider discussing your difficulties connecting with the teen with a colleague. But if, after you've received some advice and tried some engagement techniques, you still don't like the adolescent, consider referring him to another therapist. Overall, my ability to establish a solid therapeutic relationship with a teenager has always been clearly enhanced by my liking him or her.

What helps me like many of these teenage clients is an appreciation for the developmental stresses with which they are faced, as described in Chapter One. I also spend some time getting to know them and trying to find common interests or struggles, without focusing too intently in the first session on their problematic behavior. I'll talk more about this when I describe "Helpful Behaviors" in this chapter.

## Caring and Acceptance

As when working with clients of all ages, we need to care about our teenage clients sincerely and to accept them for who they are. This acceptance means that we do not feel blaming or critical of the adolescent and that we are able to honestly separate the person from his or her behavior. Troubled teens may not be able to do this themselves: they experience every hair out of place or poorly timed comment to a peer as an example of how ugly or stupid they are. And because of their egocentric nature, adolescents believe that all others—including therapists, who probably can "read their mind"—also can see these deficits.

They may also be used to being blamed by authority figures; they are waiting for it and are sensitive to it. So when working with adolescents we should be very aware of our feelings so as not to unwittingly convey criticism to the teen.

When I first began working with adolescents as a young clinician, I found it very easy to understand their struggles, and probably pushed a number of my young clients too hard to confront their parents and demand their rights as adults. After I had children of my own I developed a new insight into parenthood, and was probably more critical toward child and adolescent clients than I needed to be because I could identify with the position of their parents.

One of the things I've learned is to understand situations from everyone's point of view. I ask myself, "Why would anyone living with these parents (or in this neighborhood or with this background) respond like my young client?" I also ask myself, "Why would most parents (or teachers or friends) who interact with my teenage client respond to him this way?" By thinking about behavior as interactional, I believe I can truly understand the adolescent and anticpate how he will react to me.

I've always found that even if adolescents give me a hard time, the therapy is successful only when they can experience my caring and my sincere desire to understand their world.

## Being Familiar with Current Fads

It's helpful for us to know current fads: dress styles, musical groups, upcoming concerts, slang expressions, and so on. I don't think you should necessarily show off your familiarity with fads or try to sound or look cool, but it can aid the engagement if an adolescent client mentions a song or uses a phrase and you know about it. I recall the startled expression on thirteen-year-old Katrina's face when one day she wore an 'N Sync T-shirt, and I said, "Yeah, they're giving a concert here in July" and then sang the first line of one of their songs.

I always try to be inquisitive and intrigued about the adolescent even if I've never heard about his favorite rock group. If it comes up in conversation, or if he mentions someone or something I'm clueless about, I usually make a joke about how we "old people" aren't always up on all the new stuff, share something about what I *am* familiar with, and ask him to describe the artist or music, all with some enthusiasm and genuine interest. I may also self-disclose a little as well, talking about the music I like and what rock stars I followed when I was the client's age.

## Being Optimistic

I've supervised interns who feel very pessimistic about their young clients' ability to change. Particularly in an era of managed care, these interns believe that not much can happen in "only six sessions." Although some of this pessimism reflects their doubts about themselves as therapists, I've heard many experienced counselors express similar attitudes, because the adolescent seems so unreachable.

After thirty years of doing therapy, I'm certainly not naive enough to think there's going to be a happy ending to every story. Yet I've seen such dramatic changes occur in short periods of time that I always assume some good can come out of brief treatment.

Many times young people and their parents have remarked later on that my attitude was contagious—that they had felt pessimistic when working with other therapists who had appeared unenthused, yet had somehow felt motivated by my optimism. Optimism certainly isn't something you can just tell yourself to have, but it's useful to think in terms of, "What can I accomplish in the few sessions I have?" rather than to see the time allocated as insufficient.

# HELPFUL BEHAVIORS

It's one thing to have the requisite caring and respect for the adolescent, and another to behave in ways that convey these attitudes to the young person. Because teenagers are convinced that no one really understands them, establishing an empathic, working relationship is tricky.

Young people, particularly if they are street-smart, will see right through a sweet, "do-good" approach, and if you try this, you'll lose your credibility right away. Similarly, empathic comments that merely paraphrase content or reflect an obvious feeling are often met with rolling eyes and thoughts of, "Duh, do you really have to get a degree to learn to make such brilliant comments?" What follows, then, are some behaviors I've found helpful in engaging adolescents. As you go through these, remember that they are interventions designed not to change the teenager but rather to help establish a therapeutic bond during the first session.

## Relating in a Genuine, Down-to-Earth Manner

You can much more easily establish rapport between you and your client when you are natural and unassuming. Here's where liking teenagers and having spent time around them helps, because it gives you a sense of how to relate to the young person without pretense. Of course, we must always maintain appropriate therapeutic boundaries, so some of the same behaviors we might display to teens we're coaching on a sports team might not be useful in a counseling setting. But you'd be wise to get rid of the stiff, overly "professional" attitude that immediately creates a one-up, one-down relationship with the teen. Conducting the session in a friendly, conversational tone helps alleviate some of the young person's anxiety about counseling and helps her trust the therapist as someone who could possibly help her.

---

Robert was a sixteen-year-old client whom I initially met in juvenile hall at the request of his attorney. He'd been arrested for tagging and, when picked up by the police, was caught with marijuana. I was warned by his probation officer that Robert thought of himself as pretty hard core, and he had been in isolation during his first week of detention for hitting one of the staff members and refusing to follow procedures.

When I came to meet with him, I left all my notepads and pens in the car and convinced the staff to let me meet with Robert in the courtyard. After telling Robert that I was sent by his attorney, who was worried about how he was doing in the hall, I remarked that I was glad to meet with him outside because of the stench inside. This got him talking about the food and about what foods he missed from home. I asked him if they let him read the sports pages or watch TV, and reported to him how some professional teams and players were doing. I told Robert that part of my job was to help him figure out how he could deal with all the rules so that he could get out of detention, and that later we could talk about how he wanted to live his life so he wouldn't wind up back in juvenile hall.

## Using Humor

Using humor doesn't mean telling jokes; teens will see right through this attempt to curry their favor. Rather, it means not being too serious all the time, and reflecting on some of what the adolescent presents with some lightheartedness. Be careful not to use sarcasm or to dismiss things that the young person takes very seriously, but take a chance and share something humorous or ironic from your own experience.

For example, if a young teen comes to the session wearing a surfing shirt, I'm more likely just to make a comment about the minor liking surfing and then share a brief, funny experience I had at the beach than to ask the teen a lot of questions about his own interest in surfing. If the teen is reporting to me that he can't stand it when his mom yells, I might say, "I'll bet when she's real angry at you she uses your full name and separates the syllables, like Jon-a-than!"

Some highly resistant teens won't acknowledge my comments in this first session, but I've found, for most adolescents, that my using humor helps establish a sort of camaraderie and opens up the young person to reflect on life's ironies in later sessions.

## Self-Disclosing

I talked about therapist self-disclosure in Chapter Three, and about how we need to respect boundaries and not disclose anything that in our judgment might not be in the client's best interests or with which we're uncomfortable. Keeping this in mind, I think it's a good idea for us to disclose things about ourselves that can help the teenage client feel understood and can normalize her experience. I don't make a practice of sharing long stories or intricate details of my life, nor do I talk about how I handled a problem. What I do share are *very* brief vignettes that let the teen get to know me a little and capture the essence of what she is saying.

For example, I might volunteer times when I broke the rules or fell asleep in class or didn't tell the whole truth. I never make up a story. Sometimes I find that a bond is established even if I relate an incident that's not exactly the same as that of the client. To a thirteen-year-old who was referred for fighting and who told me that all the other kids were "dorks," I confessed that I, too, had a hard time fitting in when I was in the seventh grade. With a shy fifteen-year-old who didn't go out with peers very much, I mentioned going to a lot of movies by myself when I was a kid, which opened up a wonderful conversation about her wishing she were a heroine in a Hollywood love story.

## Not Asking Too Many Questions

Most adolescents feel scrutinized enough by their parents and teachers; they don't need another adult to ask them lots of questions. In a sense, not asking questions runs counter to what most of us are taught to do in an initial session. But let's remember that if you push the adolescent away, there won't be a second session! So even if you aren't getting all the information you'd like to get in a first session, let it go. Keep in mind that through responding to your self-disclosures or to comments you make about the process, the teen will reveal lots of valuable information *without* your asking a lot of questions. For example, many teens will hear me tell a brief story about my life, and respond by telling me a story about their own lives.

I find it more helpful to opening up a nondefensive discussion for me to make declarative statements. For example, I might comment that the adolescent "looks pissed off" about being here, or say "I'd be pretty pissed off if that happened to me," or even "Most kids your age would be pissed off," rather than ask a number of open-ended, "How did that make you feel?" type questions. Again, not all adolescents will respond to this approach, and some will resist *any* of our attempts that feel as though we are putting words in their mouths. But many do respond well, continue exploring issues, and feel that we understand them.

## Not Talking Too Much About Feelings

As with not asking a lot of questions, not talking too much about feelings is the opposite of what we have been trained to do with adults. Most mental health professionals understand that feelings are intricately tied to behavior, and they know how important it is to the progress of therapy that clients become aware of their feelings. But our adolescent clients don't always know this, and even if they did, they typically have a hard time being aware of their feelings and seeing the link between the feelings and their behavior.

For many adolescents, attending to feelings is threatening. At this stage of their lives, they're bombarded with all kinds of new impulses and feelings, and they're very confused about all this. When we point out the young person's feelings, the teen may get defensive and may deny having the feelings. I remember saying to sixteen-year-olds things like, "You look upset," to which they would defensively respond with variations of "I'm not upset—I just wish everyone would stop bugging me and leave me alone." (Sounds upset to me!) I generally don't push it in the early sessions—what's important is that young clients feel understood, even if they won't verbally agree with my description.

Sometimes it has seemed to me that teenagers just refuse to acknowledge that I might be right, and have to define the world in their own terms. "I'm not sad," said a seventeen-year-old. "It's just that my whole world is falling apart." "I don't need to get no revenge," a gang member once told me; "it's like, if some dude messes with me, I'm gonna mess with him."

I understand this kind of response as their needing to protect their autonomy, and I don't get into a power struggle over words. If teens repeatedly deny feelings, I avoid pressuring them to express their emotions and I move directly into talking about their life.

## Talking About the Client's Life

Although identifying a problem and specifying a goal for therapy are important parts of the first session, the initial contact is not the time to push the young person to reveal too much, particularly about painful or embarrassing topics. Instead, talk more about the teenager's life; allowing him to talk about what he feels like talking about, and responding with genuine interest, generally goes a long way toward establishing rapport. Despite the urge to do so, don't interpret what the adolescent is saying, don't ask many intrusive questions, and in the first session you definitely shouldn't try to get the adolescent to see the errors in his thinking or behavior.

Experience and clinical judgment will help you decide just how far you can go. Some teens who mention their parents' divorce, having to move to a new part of town, and having to leave their dog behind can tolerate you saying, "Wow, you've had a lot of losses recently," whereas others will tell you to "stop analyzing them." With either kind of teen, in the first session I'm more likely to say that she's had a number of "changes" in her life and then go on to have her tell me what her new house, school, and neighborhood are like, rather than go into much depth about her pain. As suggested earlier, I might disclose that I know what it's like to lose a pet, or comment that most kids feel like they don't have much of a choice when their parents divorce. I've had too many adolescents not want to return for a second session when they've revealed too much in the first session, so I'd rather help them feel comfortable talking with me than get into too much depth right away. If it's a crisis situation, however, it's important to get down to the nitty-gritty right away, as will be discussed later in Chapter Five.

Adolescents seem to respond well to an adult showing interest in their lives. I'm curious about what they like to do, whom they spend time with, what music they listen to, and whom they feel they can talk to. I allow myself to be genuinely enthusiastic about what they tell me, and I try to remember specifics in future sessions, conveying the message that I've really listened to them. I also don't let silences go too long in the early session; I'm not suggesting that you get into a question-and-answer routine, but when silences occur you can encourage the young person to talk more about aspects of his life.

## Being Very Selective About Challenging or Confronting

Adolescents can be pretty resistant in a first session; their behavior can range from complete silence, to passive-aggressive behavior such as rolling of eyes or saying they haven't heard you, to direct hostility. As well, when they do talk about their lives, they are experts at rationalizing their actions or just plain lying. The temptation for many therapists is to confront them with their behavior, in the hope that the young person will recognize the impact she has on others and acknowledge the truth. My advice for the initial session? Be *very* selective about confronting teens in this way, as doing so can feel rejecting to the teenager and be damaging to the therapeutic relationship.

Experts recommend a basic rule of "confronting only as much as you have supported," and I agree.[3] Until the therapeutic relationship is somewhat solidified, I do a *lot* more supporting than confronting. When I do challenge the adolescent, I always try to do so in the context of support. I might say, "I'm really interested in what you're saying about your teachers, but I don't know what to make of it when you roll your eyes in here." I may also try to take responsibility for some of the teenager's reactions. For example, I might say, "When you yell at me like that, I think I probably pushed you too hard. Maybe we should drop this topic for now and come back to it later."

When it's obvious to me that the teenager is rationalizing or lying, I try to empathize with the motive behind the reported behavior rather than challenge it. To a thirteen-year-old who reported that the kid he beat up deserved it for teasing him, I'm more likely in the first session to say something like, "You must have been pretty sick and tired of taking that crap from him," rather than immediately challenge his blame-the-victim thinking. To a fourteen-year-old who tells me that she got all A's on her report card (despite her parents having told me that she failed two courses), I might say, "I know how good it feels to accomplish something and to have others be proud of me."

Does *not* confronting the lying tell the teen that he can continue to lie to you? I don't think so—not if you've captured what he's trying to tell you by his lying. Novice therapists tend to worry about this; more experienced clinicians know that, in some sense, clients never lie—they're always telling us something truthful about themselves, but we need to look at the process, not the content.

For example, if an adolescent tells me about all his sexual conquests, he may be telling me he has shallow relationships, or that he doesn't know how to establish relationships on any other basis than sex, or that he doesn't feel he has much to offer except sex. He may also be telling me that he wants to impress me, wants to avoid talking about certain topics, or is afraid to be vulnerable with me. Does it matter whether he actually did have all those sexual conquests? Not to me—and not to the success of the therapy!

One category of behaviors that warrants some heavier confrontation in the first session is crises, such as self-destructive behavior (for example, attempted suicide) or incredibly poor judgment (for example, unprotected sex with multiple partners). As in the case of lying, I empathize with the motive (for example, "Things must seem pretty hopeless right now for you to consider suicide"), but in these cases I confront the behavior as illogical, irrational, untimely, or just plain dumb!

---

Being careful not to sound Pollyannaish, I challenged a fourteen-year-old girl who considered suicide her only alternative. "From talking with your family, I think a lot of people would be upset if you were dead, including me. Seems that those people haven't done a good job of letting you know how much you mean to them—maybe that's something I can help them with."

---

To a fifteen-year-old who promised to run away as soon as she got out of the hospital, I said, "That sounds kinda dumb to me. I know you hate being home with your mom, and if half of what you say is true, I wouldn't want to be there either. But if you run away, she'll be in that nice warm apartment and you'll be trying to find a place to crash. Every time you've run away before has only gotten you in

worse trouble; last time you even wound up in here! Plus, you'll
only prove your mom right—that you weren't adult enough to work
this out."

## Validating the Adolescent

Just as they are concerned about how to respond to apparent lying,
new counselors are sometimes worried that empathizing with the
adolescent's feelings or motive is tantamount to giving them permission to continue their misbehavior. What I try to help therapists
see is the difference between agreeing with teens and validating
them. For example, if minors complain about their parents, my
responding, "You must think your parents don't understand you at
all," or "I know a lot of kids who would think their parents didn't
have a clue if they did that" is very different than my saying,
"Sounds like your parents are pretty stupid." Even if the teen asks
me something directly—for example, "Don't you think my parents
are stupid?"—I can answer, "Given all the things you say they've
done to you, I can see where you'd think that."

Sure, some teens will go home and tell their parents that even
the therapist thinks they (the parents) are worthless; but even if you
don't say anything at all about the parents, or say that you don't
even know the parents enough to comment on their behavior, these
adolescents might still claim to the adults that you said the same
thing. The key point is that it is particularly important in the first
session for the young person to feel heard and understood. Through
making empathic comments, normalizing some of her behaviors,
and self-disclosing some of our own experiences, we let the adolescent know that even the worst of her behaviors is understandable.
Even when what teens do is not good for themselves or for others,
they need some validation that there is a good reason for their
behavior.

If conveyed properly, validating the teen isn't interpreted as
license to continue the behavior. If we can capture the positive
motive behind the behavior, then the teen can feel a connection

to us. In responding to a teen in a detention center bragging about having severely beaten another kid, a counselor might say, "I see where respect is very, very important to you." To an adolescent who has intentionally cut herself, a therapist can reflect how much pain the young person is willing to endure just so she can feel something.

## Reframing: Putting the Problem in Solvable Terms

Adolescents and their families always have their own understanding of the presenting problem. Often, the parents and the teen have very different explanations for the behavior; thus, the solution proposed by the adults may be dramatically different than the solution proposed by the adolescent. Sometimes, the explanation (or framing) of the behavior makes the solution difficult, if not impossible. Part of our job in the first session is to redefine the problem so that a solution becomes possible.

---

A few years ago, parents brought in their thirteen-year-old son, Ben, who they caught sneaking out in the middle of the night to smoke marijuana with his friends. He had maintained his grades, though he was having trouble getting up in the mornings and often got to school late. He also locked himself in his room a lot and sometimes didn't want to come out and have dinner with the family; if they refused to let Ben take the food back into his room, he just didn't eat. The parents were firm in their resolve: he must stop using drugs!

Ben heard what they said in the initial family session. He looked at them, looked at me, and said, "Forget it. There's no way I'm going to stop smoking weed, so you can just save your money right now." Everyone looked at me: Which side was I going to take? Clearly, this was a setup for therapeutic failure. If I agreed that Ben should stop using marijuana, he'd never trust me; yet if I said it was OK for him to keep smoking pot, I'd lose the parents. What's a therapist to do?

What I said in this case was, "It's pretty clear you've reached an impasse on this. I'll bet you [the parents] feel like you've tried everything to get through to Ben but that nothing seems to have worked. What I can see is how concerned you are, because not only is Ben smoking marijuana, but his eating and sleeping habits have changed, and I'm sure you're scared knowing he left the house in the middle of the night. Let me meet alone with Ben for a time or two so that I can find out what he thinks about all this."

When I met with Ben, I told him that I wanted to hear his side of the story and that I would try to advocate for him to get his parents to understand him better, and maybe he and I could figure out strategies to get his parents to compromise a little. Ben said that his parents didn't give him any respect, and we agreed that he and I would work on ways to convince his parents to give him the respect he deserved.

The problem was now reframed. It was not that he smoked pot but that he had to find ways to get respect from his parents. Part of doing so, in later sessions, was for Ben to gain some awareness that his smoking pot, and all the behaviors that went with it, were sure ways not to get respect.

---

Reframing, then, is a way to engage the adolescent by putting the "problem" in his or her terms. Young people may not be motivated to stop smoking pot or to change their group of friends or to be more considerate of their parents. They might, however, buy into such goals as getting their parents not to yell at them so much, negotiating a later curfew, or having some privacy in their room. Adolescents are much more likely to cooperate with therapists who are able to incorporate the teen's goals into the treatment. So we need to present ourselves as willing to advocate for the minor, and discuss with the young person reasonable, concrete goals.

Much of what I try to do is to reframe the problem in interpersonal terms. "My parents bug me" is reframed as "Your parents haven't found a good way to express their worry about you." "Our son is disrespectful" might be reframed as "When he tries to get you to see that he's not a kid anymore, he does so in a way that turns you off." Describing the problem in an interpersonal framework immediately acknowledges that I think everyone needs to change and opens up several possibilities for later intervention.

Skillful reframing gives some focus to future sessions, instills some hope in the adolescent, and allows us to honestly support the minor and intercede on her behalf. The goals become more meaningful for the teenager, and typically she is then more willing to put some effort into figuring out ways to achieve them.

## Making the Adolescent an Expert at Problem Solving

Because adolescents typically don't ask for counseling and may not believe they need advice (certainly not from a "shrink"), they may not engage with a therapist who presents as too much of a "helper." One of the ways to deal with this is to use some of the initial session to make adolescents experts at solving their own problems. I sometimes start sentences with "You know yourself best," or "You probably know your parents better than anybody," and then have the teen brainstorm some possible first steps toward resolving a problem.

---

CJ was a fourteen-year-old boy living with his grandparents and referred for counseling after being picked up for a curfew violation. Whereas his grandparents listed a number of concerns they had about CJ, CJ's only initial goal was to "get them off my back."

In my first session with CJ, we talked some about when and where his grandparents were "on his back," and I told him that one of my roles was to see if I could help him figure out how to get more freedom in ways that wouldn't worry his grandparents. "You know them much better than I do," I said. "What kinds of things would they like to see you do that would help them not worry about you?" After a few minutes of denying that there was anything he could do, CJ was able to focus on such things as staying home on school nights, calling if he was going to be late, and leaving his door open a crack unless he needed some privacy for a while. We spent future sessions working on how he could actually do these things without feeling embarrassed or controlled and on how the grandparents could change so as to make it easier for CJ to comply with their rules.

## Educating the Adolescent About Therapy

Unlike adults, who may have a concept of what therapy is all about, adolescents may have either misconceptions about the process or no idea about the nature of counseling at all. Describe your role as someone who talks with kids, helps them understand their problems or why others think they have problems, and helps them figure out what they might want from life and how to get it. Inquire about their picture of therapy and clarify any confusion they may have.

Working from a psychoeducational framework is particularly useful in a first session with a minority adolescent. That is, explain to the young person what you'll be doing and how it will help him. You don't want to appear too intrusive, so explain why you're asking personal questions.[4] More will be said about working with adolescents from different cultures in Chapter Six.

# ENGAGING THE PARENTS

Because most adolescents still live with their parents, it is essential that we intervene not only at the individual level of the teenager but also at the contextual level of the family. Whether you conceptualize the young person's problems as primarily stemming from intrapsychic conflicts, from interpersonal relationships in the teen's life, or from an interaction of several variables, effective treatment must take into account the contributions of the young person's family to the development, maintenance, and resolution of the issues.

Thus, engaging with the parents must also occur at the beginning of therapy.

Enlisting the participation of the parents isn't easy. By the time an adolescent winds up in counseling, her parents may have given up on her or feel hopeless about their child's ability to change. They may have had unsuccessful experiences in therapy before or believe they've tried everything and that nothing works. Some are afraid to be blamed for their teenager's difficulties and don't want anyone telling them how to raise their child. Still others aren't sure why they need to attend sessions, as in their view it is the adolescent who has the problem.

Parents often feel they are in a Catch-22 situation. They don't know how to help their son or daughter, yet accepting help from a counselor makes them feel even more inadequate as parents. And, similar to an individual who fears the unknown, parents feel some ambivalence about their child's changing, because they don't know what to expect, and, in addition, change in one family member's behavior will necessitate an adjustment in everyone else's behavior.

Understanding what it must be like for parents to bring their child to a counselor can go a long way toward engaging them. Put yourself in their shoes—they've raised this adolescent for many years and tried to do their best, and now the teen's problems force them to question how good a job they've actually done. And they have many other aspects of their lives with which to deal—jobs, finances, other kids, adult relationships, and the like.

The parents have to devote extra time, money, and effort to the teen. They don't want to be blamed for their child's problems, and may be so concerned with keeping the rest of their life on track that the prospect of having to make changes seems overwhelming. We need to keep in mind that these parents are not necessarily bad parents, and that they need to be engaged in the therapeutic process as much as their adolescent.

The sections that follow describe ways we can facilitate engagement with parents.

## Assuming the Parents Want to Help

I always begin my work with adolescents by assuming that the parents love their child and are motivated to do what is in the teen's best interests. Thus, I view any "resistance" on their part as reflecting the overwhelming sense of frustration and hopelessness they must feel. It has been very useful for me to assume that they have tried their best to help the youngster and have not felt much success or appreciation for their efforts, and I tell them so.

I empathize with their deep sense of despair, anger, or guilt, to let them know that I understand what they've been through. I normalize their frustration and frame it as something felt by most parents who are passionately concerned about their kids. I acknowledge their current life stresses and how dealing with the additional stress of the teenager can't be easy. I emphasize that their teen is at a critical point in her life and that I'll need their help in understanding the young person and in coming up with new strategies to influence her.

## Educating the Parents About Developmental Norms and About Therapy

Some parents are naive about normal adolescent development and would benefit from us putting the young person's behavior into perspective so they don't overreact or underreact. For example, you may want the parents to find ways to stay out of power struggles with their child, but in order for parents to back away from a potential confrontation with their child, you may need to help them understand that attempts at engaging parents in power struggles are inevitable for many teens and may not signal the beginning of a downward spiral into delinquency. Educating parents in this way also instills some hope and makes it easier for them to engage in the therapeutic process. I try to counter any beliefs they may have about their inability to influence their child by referring to developmental literature that has shown that although teens may not need parents the way they did when they were younger, they still need parents.[5]

Parents also benefit from our explanations of how therapy works. For example, parents find it enormously reassuring to hear that I won't focus on who's at fault for the teen's problem or on the mistakes they may have made as parents. Because they may wonder how much I'm going to ask of them, I detail the structure of treatment, explaining that I am interested in meeting primarily with the adolescent but that I also plan to have an occasional family session if some parent-child issue comes up and even, perhaps, a session alone with the parent or parents if I need their assistance in helping the teen.

## Focusing on a Solvable Problem

As I do with the adolescent, I try to help the parents choose a focus for the treatment, one that is clear and phrased in terms of a solvable problem. Like all clients, parents of teens can be more engaged in therapy and willing to participate if they know what the goals are and know what to look for. So, for example, "Improvement in my child's self-esteem" might be replaced by "My child spending more time with friends" or "No running away."

One of our main tasks is to frame the problem as one over which the adolescent has some control and one that the parents can influence. Because it's very likely we'll be asking the parents to change some of their interactions with the teen, the problem must be defined in such a way that they can understand why *their* change will evoke a change in their child. If a problem is defined as purely medical or as something beyond the control of the adolescent and the family, then gaining the family's cooperation in trying any new behaviors becomes a difficult task.

As mentioned earlier, I try to reframe the problem for the parent as having an interpersonal component. I might use the concept that "children often seem deaf to their parents" as a way to invite the parents in future sessions to find new ways to communicate so that the child can "hear" them. If parents attribute the minor's behavior to a character flaw in the young person, I might say, "Particularly in cases where the teenager's behavior reflects some personality problem, we find that what's necessary to solve the problem is for the more reasonable people in his life to model more appropriate behaviors for him so that he can learn from them."

While reframing in the preceding way might seem duplicitous, we must remember that diagnosing a problem from a particular theoretical perspective is always a hypothesis; that is, a diagnosis is merely a way to understand a behavior. Calling a behavior a "character flaw" is as valid as calling it a "parent/child" problem, and the framing of the problem should always lead to a treatment plan. Framing the problem in an interpersonal way helps to not only engage the adolescent and his parents, but also to develop an intervention strategy based on interpersonal goals.

———————

At the beginning of the chapter, I reiterated how critically important it is to establish a solid working relationship with teenagers. Although this is often not an easy process, following some of the guidelines I described can enable you to engage the adolescent and his or her parents and to gain credibility and trust.

In Chapter Five I'll describe the actual process of the first session, showing you how to put into practice some of the attitudes and behaviors I discussed in Chapter Four.

# 5

# The Process of the First Session

We need always try to keep in mind that although the first session may be therapeutic in many ways, the goals of the initial contact are to engage the adolescent and his family, reduce any negative expectations about therapy they might have, and set the tone and parameters for future sessions. The goals may be a bit different in a crisis situation, but generally I've found that focusing on relationship building in the initial session goes a long way.

The first session is also a diagnostic one—not in the sense of our giving tests or taking a detailed history, but in terms of getting a picture of who our client is and how she relates. How does the adolescent behave toward her parents? Is she outgoing or reserved? Does she seem bright and motivated? Scared? Unhappy? Anxious? Sad? Does the teen behave in age-appropriate ways, or does she seem much younger or older? Does she have an understanding of the problem, even if it's a different understanding than that of the parents? How does the young person seem to feel about herself?

Answers to these and other questions emerge primarily from the context of the first session. We also have the information provided by the referral source so we can begin to generate hypotheses about the adolescent that we can test out in future sessions. As stated in Chapters One and Two, we need to compare the adolescent's behavior (both within the first session and from information secured from the referral source) to developmental norms so that we can formulate an accurate diagnosis and create an appropriate treatment plan.

## The Initial Telephone Call

If an initial telephone call comes from a parent, I ask that person for a brief description of the *current* problem, where the referral is coming from (for example, school, parent, adolescent, police, and so on), and who is in the family. Even this minimal information gives me some thoughts about the nature of the presenting problem and helps me prepare for the first session.

For example, if it appears that the teen is in a crisis, such as threatening suicide, I get the family to bring the teen in within twenty-four hours—if I can't schedule a session that quickly in an emergency situation, I tell the parent that it sounds as if the minor should be seen immediately, and I make some referrals to other clinicians and the crisis hotline, with a request that the parent call me back to let me know the family has made contact with another therapist.

If the presenting problem doesn't seem to be a crisis, I tell the parent that I have found it best to meet with the family as a whole for the first session so that I can get an understanding of how everyone perceives the problem and is affected by it. If the parent protests that it's the teenager's problem, not theirs, I reassure them that my intent in having everyone come in is not to find out whose fault it is but to have everyone tell me his or her story, because family members often have a more accurate picture of what's going on than does the teenager. Besides, I may need their help in the future in supporting the teen's changes.

If the parent asks me what to tell the teen, I always advocate telling the truth, which can be a simple statement, such as, "I'm concerned and worried about the fact that your grades have been slipping, and have made an appointment with a therapist so we can all talk about this and try to come up with ways to help you get back on track." Any further questions the teen might ask the parent, such as what the length of treatment is or what exactly the therapist will be doing, should be answered with, "I don't know. But let's ask him when we see him."

If teenagers call directly, I try to get a sense of whether they are self-referred or are calling because their parents made them do so. In the former situation, I generally respect their request, tell them I'd be happy to meet them so we can talk at length about what's troubling them, and schedule an appointment. Because there are legal issues related to seeing a minor, as discussed in Chapter Three, I ask them to bring a parent or legal guardian with them so that that person can sign the authorization forms—though if the teen is reluctant to do so, I agree that we'll talk about this at the first session.

If it appears that the young person is being coerced to call, I prefer to have the whole family come in for the first session. As described earlier, I tell the teen that I have found it best for me to meet with everyone so as to get each person's ideas about the problem and then to follow up with an individual appointment for the adolescent. I make a tentative appointment for the whole family and tell the teen to check out if this is an OK time for everyone and to call me back. I take the teen's phone number as well and will call her back if I haven't heard from her in a couple of days; I do this in case the adolescent is afraid to involve the family or if the family refuses to come in and the teen is embarrassed to call and tell me. If this turns out to be the case, I'll set a time for an individual appointment with the minor, saying, "Let's you and I go ahead and meet, and we can talk about whether or not to bring your family in at a later point."

Sometimes the referral comes from a nonfamilial person. Staff or probation officers at juvenile hall might ask you to see the minor, teachers or a principal might send a teen to the counselor's office, or a hospital practitioner may be referred a case from a physician or psychiatrist. In these circumstances, the ideal process would be for you to have a brief meeting with the teenager and the referring person first, so that the referring person can explain to you in front of the minor why the referral is being made. If this is impractical, I'd advise you to at least have a talk with the referring person before seeing the adolescent, so that you can get a clear picture of the presenting issue and of what the referring person wants from you.

## Meeting with the Parents

Some clinicians routinely meet with the parents first, in order to get a developmental history of the minor and begin to formulate a diagnostic impression. I prefer not to do so, for several reasons:

- Getting lots of details about the teen before we've met biases my perceptions when I actually do meet him for the first time, and I find I'm more likely to interpret the young person's behavior through these filters.

- As a more systemically oriented therapist, I consider seeing the parents first in order to understand the minor as similar to trying to understand how a car works by looking at the spark plugs—the whole is always more than the sum of the parts.

- For me, assessment is part of an ongoing process, not something that happens *before* treatment begins. I've found it much more helpful in my work to get historical information when it's relevant to what we're discussing, in the same way that a person will learn much more effectively how to do therapy if she allows her questions to emerge from the practice rather than tries to learn everything about the process before engaging in it.

- I don't find factual data about the adolescent as helpful as process data—that is, *how* the young person behaves, *how* the parents react, *who* gets involved in trying to help the teen, and so on. Certainly some factual data are important in making a differential diagnosis, but they may not be as critical as process data and can be obtained later.

- I've found that teenage clients are pretty mistrustful once they find that the therapist has had extensive contact with the parents. Clinicians then start off having to prove to the minor that they're not agents of the parents.

So I definitely prefer to meet with the entire family first—or at least with the adolescent first if bringing in the whole family isn't feasible—and to get diagnostic information in front of the teenager or, with some rationale given, from the parents in a subsequent session.

## Beginning the Initial Session with the Entire Family

The initial session with the family begins in the waiting room. Parents are given an Informed Consent document and Consent to Treat Minors form they are asked to read and sign, and the minors are given an Assent to Treatment document that covers some of the same information as the Informed Consent form.

When I go to the waiting room, I try to be warm and friendly, yet professional. I introduce myself as "Dr. Ribner" as I shake hands first with the parents, then with the children in roughly chronological order. If the grandparents are present, I will address them first. With younger children or early adolescents, I bend over or kneel to their level and try to say something engaging. For example, I might comment on the toys they're playing with or the book they're reading in the waiting room, or the sports team logo on their shirt, or I even ask if they came to the appointment straight from school. I'll do the same with the older adolescent if the situation presents itself, but I won't stretch to find something to comment on—shaking the teen's hand and saying, "Nice to meet you" may be enough.

Although I'm not overly formal, I think it's important to introduce myself as "Dr. Ribner" rather than "Neil Ribner" when working with children or adolescents. I want the teen to know this is a serious process and that I'm someone with some training and expertise rather than a peer. Introducing myself in a more formal way also seems to help me gain some credibility with the parents, who want to see me as an expert who can help their child.

Why greet the parents or grandparents first? Doing so is respectful and culturally appropriate, and supports generational boundaries. Doing so indicates my awareness of who are the authorities and caregivers in the family, and helps the parents feel connected to me. Engaging the minor immediately afterwards, or what Minuchin calls "joining," establishes a connection between the young person and me and encourages the child or adolescent to see me as a benign, friendly figure; and if the parents see that I am warm and bonded with their child, they're likely to be more trusting of me and hopeful that we will be able to make some progress.[1]

When the family enters the office, I encourage them to sit anywhere they'd like (except in my chair, on which I've placed a clipboard or some papers to indicate that that's where I sit). I begin to note possible family alignments by observing where family members sit, but I don't comment on them right away. If any family members are absent, despite my having made clear over the phone that I'd like to see everyone, I comment that "someone seems to be missing." I ask what happened with the absent member and comment that "we'll have to see about including them in the future."

In the spirit of joining and establishing rapport, I start the session by acknowledging the phone call I got from one of the parents or the teen and say, "I'd like to know a little about each of you—who would like to start?" I then wait to see who begins, or, if the tension mounts, I will ask one of the adults to begin. Because it's critical to establish a bond with the authorities in the family, I make a special effort to reach out to those persons. If family members immediately go into the presenting problem, though, I tell them that "we'll get to that in a little bit—tell me something about yourself first." Although this might sound a little like I'm avoiding the problem, the rapport established through this process is important, and the family is typically reassured by the fact that I'm adding structure to the session.

As the family members share things with me, I can empathize, show interest, and even reveal some personal snippets in order to help them feel safe. I make sure everyone in the family gets a turn, encourage people to speak for themselves, and allow them to say anything they want to, but I won't push too hard if someone refuses. In those instances, I might say, "That's fine; sometimes it's hard to get started. Maybe we can come back to you later."

## Identifying the Problem

After I've met everyone, I say, "I'd like to find out from everyone what problems brought you in here today and how I can help." I again wait for a response or ask the person who called me to share her thoughts with the rest of the family. Typically, a parent will answer, "We're here because of Hector" and will go on to complain about the adolescent's behavior. It's important at this point to help the parent operationalize her concern. So if she answers in a vague way, such as "Hector is depressed" or "Hector isn't respectful," I ask her how the young person "shows" his depression or his disrespect. The parent might, for example, describe that the teenager stays in his room all day, hardly eats anything, or doesn't go out with friends. She might state that the young person slams doors, or curses at them when asked to do chores.

I discourage others from interrupting or defending themselves, telling them that "everyone will have their turn." I also don't let one person talk for too long, as I want everyone to have a chance to share his or her side of the story. After a person has stated a few specific behaviors that concern him, I ask him how he has been affected by the behaviors, empathize with his struggle, and ask him for his understanding of the reasons for the problem and what he has tried to do to solve it.

I have each member of the family likewise detail for me what she sees the problem to be, her reactions to it, her understanding of the reasons for the problem, and her previous attempts to find a solution. Clearly, much of the time the adolescent sees the problem very differently than do the parents—in this first session your job is not to resolve the problem, so you must resist family members' attempts to get you to take sides by agreeing with them. My purpose at this point in the session is for everyone to lay her cards on the table, for me to show each person that I respect her point of view and can understand her side of it, and to begin to formulate some goals and a strategy for accomplishing those goals.

Reframing the problem such that it is solvable, as discussed earlier, is very helpful here. I try to take the problem out of the "unsolvable" category and define it as one that is treatable with therapy and that will respond to changes by the youth and the parents. I often will frame the issue in interpersonal terms: "Erin won't stop misbehaving" becomes "You haven't been able to get her to see the seriousness of her behavior." "Todd is depressed" might be reframed as, "Todd is probably unhappy about some things in his life and hasn't found a good way, yet, to get the family's help with figuring these things out."

As I listen to each person, I'm trying to get a clearer picture of the context of the presenting problem: When and where does it occur? With whom? How do family members understand the problem? How do they get involved in trying to solve the problem? What happens that helps the problem *not* occur? How will everyone know the problem is solved?

As each person is sharing his perspective, I also make a mental note of others' reactions. I wait to comment on these, however, as I want each person to tell his story and feel that I am listening and understand, without too many interruptions or distractions. I make certain I empathize with each person, particularly around his desire to reach and help his child (even if he is going about it in ineffective or inappropriate ways).

## Establishing Therapeutic Guidelines

There are certain interactional guidelines I promote in this session. I certainly want to see how the family members relate to each other, so I let their interactions proceed as usual up to a point. But if the anger and blaming become pronounced, I'll usually reframe the "passion" that everyone feels about the issue and tell the family that I want to use the session to get their perspective on the problem first, before we try to resolve the issue.

In this way, I set a guideline that I won't allow the adolescent to get scapegoated in the session. I don't merely state this at the beginning of treatment because I want to see what the family usually does before I intervene. But it's not useful for us to allow a family to spend the first session doing just what they do back home.

I also resist doing things that the parents should be doing without first giving them an opportunity to do it. I establish a guideline that, although I'm here to help, I'm not the parent and I won't take over for the parent. For example, if the younger kids are climbing on the furniture or throwing things at each other, I wait to see how the parents deal with it; then I might ask the parents to get the kids to sit quietly, rather than ask the youngsters to quiet down myself. If the parents seem clueless, though, I'll intervene so as to control the order and then talk to the parents about this at a later session.

Another major category of behavior I won't allow is parental discussion of adult issues in front of the children. Sometimes it becomes apparent in their discussing the adolescent's problem that the parents disagree, and they may start putting each other down. "If you'd make the family a priority, maybe the kids wouldn't act that way," says mom. "Well, if you wouldn't let them get away with so much, and would clean the house every now and then, I wouldn't feel like staying away so much," answers dad. When the apparent marital issues come up, or when a single parent criticizes the child's other parent, I say, "These sound like adult issues—let's plan on meeting at another time without the kids so we can talk about these issues." Our setting such hierarchical boundaries can be therapeutic in itself and serves as necessary modeling for the family.

### Encouraging Interaction Among Family Members

After all family members have given their view of the problem, I make a strategic decision: I can encourage the family to interact around the issue presented, or I can ask the other family members to let me have some time alone with the adolescent. The general guideline for making this decision is as follows: I meet alone with the adolescent if, in my judgment, she feels isolated, scapegoated, and unsupported or if I don't feel I've made a reasonably strong connection with her. Remembering that a main goal of the initial session is to establish a working relationship with the adolescent, I don't want the session to end with the young person feeling distant from me and hopeless about the process.

If my sense is that the teenager feels some connection to me and to the family and is engaged in the therapeutic process so far, then it's safe to encourage some interaction. With some quiet families, I ask them to pick an example of their interactions around the presenting problem (for example, what they've done when the teenager walks in late) and to show me what happens, consistent with Minuchin's technique of "enactment."[2] I observe the process and try to understand how the family interactions are related to the presenting problem.

With most families, though, I merely comment that they seem stuck, that they seem to have quite different ideas about what the problem is, or that they look like they had reactions to each other's comments; I then encourage them to talk to each other about their different ideas about the problem or their reactions to each other. As I do when I suggest an enactment, I watch for how family members interact, how they communicate, and how they express their feelings, but, because this is the first session, I'm more likely to comment on their positive actions—such as how hard they're trying to communicate with each other—than on their negative ones. I also summarize their positions and goals; for example: "Mom, what you'd like to see is Janet getting better grades and interacting more with her friends"; "Dad, you'd like it if Janet went with you for a walk once or twice a week"; "Billy, you want your parents to stop yelling so much and maybe for your dad to spend more time with you"; "Janet, you'll know things are changing if your parents don't bug you so much, and maybe if they extended your curfew once in a while on a Friday night."

I also won't let people speak for other people in the session. If I ask the teenager for his opinions and mom or dad speak, I say, "I'd like everyone to speak for themselves. People in families often have different views, and it's important that I get everyone's unique perspective." Another thing I do is to reframe any initial signs of despair or hopelessness by saying something like, "Things you have tried *so far* haven't worked"; normalize that "many families feel pretty overwhelmed when they begin therapy"; and add that "my job is to help *everyone* in the family feel more content and satisfied with their lives."

## Seeing the Adolescent Alone

If I see the adolescent alone for a while, I immediately start with a strong statement of support.

---

In a first family session, Kavitha, a sixteen-year-old East Indian girl, had endured twenty minutes of criticism from both her parents. They told her how ashamed they were of her, called her names like "slut," and threatened to send her to live with relatives if she didn't start showing them proper respect. Kavitha didn't defend herself, said she had nothing to say when asked her view of the problem, and the only expression of feeling she let out was a tear or two.

When her parents left for the waiting room, I said to her, "Wow! I feel terrible for you! I can only imagine how it must feel to listen to so much criticism and not feel like you can say anything back." Kavitha's tears began to flow, and she started telling me how alone she felt and how terrified she was that her parents would actually send her to her relatives to live.

---

In another case, fourteen-year-old Sean, his mother, stepfather, and nine-year-old sister were in the first session. Sean had gotten suspended for fighting at school a second time and was likely to be expelled if it happened again. His mom was very passive, deferring her authority to her new husband. (They had been married two years.) To make matters worse, Sean's sister was described as a "little angel," and both stepdad and mom kept asking Sean why he couldn't be more like her. In the initial session, stepdad blamed all the family's troubles on Sean, including the couple's growing marital problems. Sean responded in session by telling stepdad that everything was OK until he came around, which only led to stepdad's being more demeaning of him while mom sat quietly. When mom started crying, sister came over to comfort her. At this point, I asked the family to let me have a few moments alone with Sean.

Sean probably expected me to scold him like stepdad, because he seemed absolutely shocked when I said, "Boy, was that tense! If this is what happens at home, I can really understand why you're so angry and get into fights!" Sean buried his head but didn't respond. "Is this what happens?" I asked. "You get blamed for stuff, and no one's on your side?" Sean started wiping his eyes but was still silent. I added, "I'll bet it wasn't like this before your mom got remarried." That broke it—Sean just reamed the guy, explaining what a jerk he was to both him and his mom, and how angry he was at his mom for taking it.

---

Meeting alone with the teenager, even for just a few minutes, allows you to connect before the end of the initial session. It also gives the teen a chance to tell her side of the story and to enlist your aid in finding a solution. I don't guarantee adolescents that we can solve every problem to their satisfaction, but I promise to advocate for them and help them strategize ways to get what they want.

## Ending the Session

After connecting with the adolescent for a few minutes, I invite the family back in to end the session. At this point, I explain the structure of the therapy in realistic terms and clarify any misconceptions the family members might have about therapy. Whether I've seen the adolescent alone or not, I tell the family that I'd like to meet with the minor next time by himself and that I might meet with him for a few sessions before bringing the family back in. If adult or marital issues have emerged in the initial meeting, I tell the parents that "since it sounds like there may be some adult issues we need to discuss, I'd like to meet with you [adults] after I meet with the teenager once or twice. There may also be some information about your teenager that I'll want to get from you that would be boring for him to have to listen to, like his medical history."

I explain very simply that when the teen and I meet, "We'll be talking about things that are upsetting or worrisome or problematic for him, and trying to come up with some solutions. Some of the solutions might involve your [the family's] cooperation, so I'll ask you to come to a family session so we can all work things out together." I then ask if they have any questions or thoughts about the process and clarify procedures. ("No, I won't be hypnotizing your son." "No, I don't plan on having your daughter just blame you for everything—it's a much better use of everyone's time for us to focus on solving problems rather than trying to figure out whose fault they are.")

The last few minutes of the session are spent reviewing confidentiality and reporting laws. I emphasize that "for me to do my best work with the teen, both she and I need to know that except where the law requires me to break confidentiality, everything she and I talk about will be kept confidential. If I believe she's in danger, I'll let you know, and I can give you general updates about how she's doing. But it's important that you [the parents] respect her choices as to what she does or doesn't tell you about the sessions." We then review fees and insurance, and I make the appointment for the teen's individual session and give the appointment card to the adolescent.

## Conducting the First Session with the Adolescent Alone

If you've already met the teenager in the family session, you have a picture of the problem and how it affects other family members. If this is your first contact with the young person, all you have is either the brief telephone description of the problem or some referral information from another source. If you can have the referral source sit in at the beginning of the first session, do it; have the person say in front of the teen why she is making a referral, and check with the teen to make certain he understands what the referral is all about (even if he disagrees with the details). Then have that person leave, and spend the rest of the time alone with the teen.

If the referring person isn't available, at some point in the first session it's important to let the teen know what information you have and where you got it. Being honest about this helps your credibility and begins to establish you as someone working for the teen, not as an agent of the parents, school, or society. Start the session, though, by briefly introducing yourself and your role. "Manuel? Hi, I'm Dr. Smith. Let's find a place we can talk . . . I'm the school psychologist. When kids get into trouble here at school, or when the principal or a teacher is worried about a student, they ask me to talk with the student to see if I can help."

In a detention center, it might be, "Carmen? I'm Dr. Jones. I'm a psychologist for the probation department. Part of the program here is for me to meet with kids who have gotten arrested. I talk with them, find out how things are going in their lives, and see if there's any way I can help them figure things out."

As described earlier, in an attempt to build rapport I usually begin by talking about something other than the problem. "How long have you been here in juvenile hall? How are they treating you? What was your life like before you got arrested?" In a school setting, you might remark, "Did you go to the homecoming game last week? Did you hear what happened after the game?" In a psychiatric hospital, you can comment on the food or the rigid schedule, or ask the client about his or her roommate. Share something personal; for example, "I had a pretty weird roommate myself once—he used to wear the same shirt every Monday, another one every Tuesday, and so on for the rest of the week. He'd get really nervous if he forgot to wash a certain shirt before the day he was supposed to wear it."

As when you ask for family members' perspectives, the next step is to ask adolescents if they know why they're here with you. Sometimes they report the reasons pretty accurately, and you can ask follow-up questions about what they think of coming to therapy to work on these issues. Many times, they say they don't know; ask them to guess. If you still draw a blank, this is a good time to tell them about the information you got from the referral source. "Your mom called and told me she's been worried about you, that you've been sleeping a lot lately and not getting your homework done," or "I understand from your probation officer that you got picked up with a bunch of other kids near that robbery last week." These brief comments should be enough to start the conversation.

Needless to say, you should focus on helping adolescents tell their story in their own way. Remember, our job in the first session is not to interrogate the teen about "the truth." Even when I bring up information given to me by others, I try not to imply that the information is factual. For example, rather than say, "Your teacher told me how rude and disrespectful you've been to her," I'll say, "Your teacher told me she and you haven't been getting along too well lately." "I hear from your probation officer that you had a run-in with the cops last week" is better than, "I hear from your probation officer that you robbed a grocery store last week."

### Getting the Teen to Talk

What you are interested in during the first session is letting the adolescent know what information you have and giving him an invitation to talk about it. Even if the teenager denies the problem, at least he knows you are willing to talk about it. This can be particularly important if it's something embarrassing, like an eating disorder or sexual orientation confusion. The initial session is not the time to confront any apparent lying—adolescents know when they're not telling the whole truth, and they appreciate not being challenged about this right away.

Instead, point out that the teen and the referral source seem to have different opinions about the issue, and tell the teen that what you'd really like to talk about is her view. Be very sensitive at this point; don't cut off the conversation if the young person seems comfortable disclosing, but don't push for too much depth, as the teen might feel embarrassed later. I often will acknowledge how important an issue the topic is and how we should probably talk about it more in subsequent sessions; then I invite the teen to bring up any other issues she'd like to talk about.

If the adolescent brings up an issue, do a quick assessment so that you can get a picture of the context of the problem: When, where, how, and with whom does it occur? What are the accompanying symptoms, and how long has the adolescent experienced these symptoms? Do the symptoms seem to be getting better or worse, or are they staying the same? How is the teen affected by the symptoms? Has he or others done anything that seems to make the symptoms better or worse?

Most of the strategies discussed in Chapter Four in the section "Helpful Behaviors" should be used at this point. Empathize so that the young person knows you understand, but don't push for feelings too much. Reframe others' (for example, parents') behaviors as motivated out of caring and concern for the teen, even though these other people are not communicating this caring in a way the minor can feel. Share some personal information to establish rapport, even including feelings like these: "I feel scared for you when you say you drive a hundred miles an hour—I'd hate to lose you before I even got to know you!" Operationalize the teen's goals and indicate your willingness to help her figure out some strategies for accomplishing the goals, but don't give false promises or sound Pollyannaish.

### Discussing the Adolescent's World

Because I want young clients to know that I'm really interested in them and in all aspects of their lives, I usually spend a few minutes near the end of the first session having them tell me what their world is like aside from the problem. This is also a good strategy to use if the adolescent has been particularly resistant about talking about the presenting problem. If you have followed the outline I have described, and have shared with the teenager what the referral source has told you and invited her reflections on the issue, but the young person dismisses the problem or doesn't want to talk about it, it's best to say, "That's fine, we can talk about this later. Let's get to know each other a little bit first. Tell me about the other important parts of your life, like school, friends, what you like to do on weekends. . . ."

I also always include a brief discussion of the adolescent's perspectives on his family—how he gets along with family members, whom he feels close to or distant from, what his relationship with his siblings is like, how people in the family communicate, and whether there is any extended family support. One question I ask all teenagers is, "Whom in your family are you worried about?" Many will deny worrying about anyone, and I ask, "If there was someone in the family that you *would* worry about, who would it be?" In my thinking, alerting the teen to the possibility that her seemingly disruptive behavior may actually have a helpful, positive motive lays the groundwork for future family interventions.

## Concluding the Session

Whether or not you've reviewed some of the adolescent's present-ing issues, at least you've mentioned them and let the young person know you think they are important to talk about, if not in the first session then in a later one. You may also have gotten to know the teenager a bit and shared some things about yourself as a way to establish a trusting relationship.

Before the session ends, you need to review confidentiality and reporting laws. I go over these even if I've discussed them in a family session; I think it's very useful to again reassure the teen that the only time you'll break confidentiality is when required to do so by law or when you believe the adolescent is in danger. I repeat that her parents are entitled to a summary of her progress but that I'll give this summary either in a family session or after I've discussed with the teen what I'll say to the parents; either way, I won't reveal the content of our discussions unless she wants me to do so.

Because I always like to meet the teen's family at some point, I mention this: "I find it very useful in my work with teenagers to meet their families at some point, so that I can get their ideas about what the problem is and clarify what I'll be doing. It may also be that I'll want to get some information about what you were like growing up that you might have forgotten, or I might be asking them to make some changes themselves in the future. So after you and I meet a couple of times, maybe we'll talk about having them come in for a session." Also, if the parents have not signed the nec-essary paperwork, I remind the adolescent that I need them to do so and that I'll be mailing the consent forms home. I then answer any questions the young person might have about treatment, and schedule the next appointment.

# DEALING WITH CRISES

On occasion, adolescents are confronted with unexpected situational crises, such as the death of a loved one, being the victim of a crime, having been sexually assaulted, or witnessing a disaster. At these times, the teenager may be referred for crisis counseling to help him deal with the event and restore him to normal functioning. We should be prepared to see these teens in crisis centers, hospitals, detention centers, and on school campuses as well as in our offices.

In Chapter Two I discussed the symptoms we might see in adolescents exposed to trauma: shock, grief, isolation, fearfulness, and helplessness, to name a few. And whereas some complex crises will take a longer time and more frequent sessions, most teens in crisis situations respond well to a model that emphasizes support and mutual problem solving, such as that proposed by Rusk.[3] The basic approach is to help the teen manage the symptoms of the crisis, feel safe both emotionally and physically, and secure needed support.

---

Justin was a fifteen-year-old who I saw several years ago when I did some consulting work in a local high school. He came in on emergency, saying that he had just found out that his girlfriend, Carla, was sneaking around behind his back with his good friend Matt. He was clearly very anxious, and he started ranting about Carla and going off into tangents about his parents' divorce and all the schoolwork he had to do. It was apparent that I had to help Justin focus, because if I let him ramble, he'd leave the session just as anxious as when he began.

I first empathized with all that was going on in his life and how overwhelmed he felt. I then told him we'd have time to figure everything out, but that right now "we need to focus on how you're going to get through the next couple of days." I asked him if he had anybody to talk to and what his schedule was like today and tomorrow. We reviewed whether he really had to take any action immediately concerning Carla or whether he could wait until we had a chance to discuss the options. Justin assured me he wasn't suicidal or homicidal, although he had some unrealistic thoughts, such as, "If Carla leaves me, I'll never have anyone love me again." I told him that when people are terribly hurt, as he was, their thinking isn't always accurate and that I could help him assess the likelihood of his conclusion about never having anyone ever love him again. Hearing that I would be there for him, he agreed that reviewing his thinking was a good idea. We then went over some ideas for distracting himself from these negative thoughts, such as keeping himself busy or writing things in a journal, and made an appointment for the next afternoon.

---

The first crisis session, then, goes beyond rapport building; you need to be very active in addressing the nature of the crisis; the disturbing thoughts, feelings, and behaviors; and possible actions the teen might take to feel more secure. Initially, you should present yourself as concerned and caring, ready to help the adolescent get through the crisis. This attitude then encourages the teenage client to share the feelings he is experiencing; when he does so, you need to express genuine caring and empathy so that the minor can feel understood and know he is not alone.

Following your expressions of caring and empathy, you and the teen should discuss what the crisis is all about and formulate possible strategies for dealing with the problem. Before the session is over, you and the client must agree on a specific strategy for managing the crisis, which might include involving other support systems, such as family and friends. The agreed-on strategy might also include medical referrals or legal action, as well as plans for follow-up counseling.

# RESISTANCE

Ideally, the hints I've presented in this chapter and in Chapter Four on engaging the adolescent and conducting the first session will allow you to establish a more effective therapeutic relationship with your young client. I'm going to end this chapter by presenting my understanding of resistance in teens and how you might deal with it.

There are many reasons why adolescents are resistant to treatment. Like all clients, teens may not want to face their problems and may be reluctant to begin a process of uncovering and talking about deep issues. Although they might be troubled by aspects of their lives, the prospect of dealing head-on with their pain and anxieties is frightening. Resisting treatment, then, is a way they protect themselves.

Another cause of resistance for all clients, including adolescents, is their sense of hopelessness about change. They may have experienced failures in their young lives; perhaps they have even been in some sort of counseling before that was ineffective. As a result of these failures, they're very cautious about trying again. Nancy Boyd-Franklin points out that this may be particularly so for clients from minority groups and disadvantaged backgrounds; they often have experienced powerlessness in dealing with social institutions and professionals, so their low motivation for therapy may reflect an experiential reality rather than a psychological issue.[4]

Teenagers may be resistant to treatment for reasons related to normal development as well. Remember the rallying cry of the 1960s? "Don't trust anyone over thirty." Adolescents may have a hard time believing that any adult can understand and help them. They may resent being forced to talk to a "shrink," and their experience with well-meaning adults has taught them that the only thing adults want is to control them and make their lives miserable. They are also pretty private; they may fear looking stupid or crazy or having their friends find out.

Another aspect of resistance concerns teenagers' need for independence. Because adolescents are typically struggling for autonomy, their radar is alert to situations that look to them as if others are asserting power or authority. Also, many teens who have been referred for treatment have had a long history of conflict with authority figures and may thus expect therapy to be another experience of an adult trying to reduce their freedom.

For all the reasons I've outlined in this section, I keep in mind that the initial session is to gain trust from the young person, not to push for "the truth" or to confront the teen in a moralizing fashion. Reframing problems so that the client can buy into the goals of counseling is also vital; doing so lets the adolescent know I'm working for her.

From a systems perspective, I always understand teens' reluctance to engage as arising partly from the goal of protecting their family from having to confront other issues, such as marital problems or psychiatric conditions in one of its members. In such situations, the minor's reluctance to be in treatment also reflects the family's ambivalence about change: at some level, everyone knows that if the adolescent begins therapy, other family secrets might be uncovered.

Resistance, then, should not be viewed with negativity, as if the adolescent were purposefully making our job difficult. Instead, we need to approach any signs of resistance with empathy and understanding, viewing the young person's reluctance to engage as motivated by a desire to protect himself or his family, as reflecting normal development, or as a realistic reaction to a series of disappointments or mistreatments by adults in authority.

All of the suggestions described in Chapter Four in the sections "Helpful Attitudes" and "Helpful Behaviors" should be considered with treatment-resistant adolescents. Sometimes it helps to acknowledge teens' resistance right up front and to make a declarative statement such as, "You must have had some pretty bad experiences with adults before to make you feel so angry about being here," or "Many of my teenage clients don't have much confidence in counseling." I usually find it helpful early in the first session to review confidentiality and to assure the minor that, except in specified legal circumstances, she is the one who decides who knows she's in therapy and what they know about it. If the counseling occurs in a more public place, such as in juvenile hall or the school counselor's office, we talk about what the minor can say to others about coming to see me, and I assure her that I won't be talking to others without her permission.

I also find it helpful to give the resistant adolescent a lot of latitude about what he discusses. As described earlier, I acknowledge what I've heard from referral sources, but I tell the teen that we don't have to talk about these issues right now if he chooses not to. I clarify my role as someone who will try to help him get what he wants and needs without putting himself or others in any danger, and try to convey that as long as he is here for a certain number of sessions, I'd like to get to know him and see if we can make some good use of our time together.

—————

At this point, you should have a clear picture of how to conduct the initial session. You'll have to develop your own style of engaging the adolescent and his family, but hopefully you now have some ideas about what might help you establish a solid working relationship.

In Chapter Six I'll discuss some special adolescent populations and what we need to consider when working with teenagers from these groups.

# 6

# Special Populations

Not all adolescents experience the world like the teens I've discussed in Chapters One and Two. Some are born with physical disabilities that make it difficult for them to meet developmental needs; others are subjected to cultural demands that lead to clashes with their peers or families, or are forced to deal with environmental pressures, such as the divorce of their parents, that add extra stress to their lives. In this chapter, I'll review some of the major issues facing adolescents who belong to special populations.

## ADOLESCENTS WITH CHRONIC DISABILITIES

Children with a chronic illness are estimated to be one-and-a-half to three times more likely than their peers to have adjustment problems.[1] When the chronic illness includes a disability, the rates are even higher for such disorders as ADHD, neuroses, social adjustment problems, and school problems.

Adolescents with disabilities must deal not only with the normal developmental tasks of the teen years but also with the extra challenges that are a part of having a chronic condition.[2] As a result, these young people tend to be more anxious, dependent, and passive, and to have a lack of confidence and a low self-esteem.[3]

Although certain characteristics might be unique to specific disabilities, research has demonstrated a higher incidence of general psychopathology in this population. Adolescents with disabilities are thus likely to present to a clinician with one or more of the following characteristics: conduct problems, anxious-withdrawn personalities, passivity-inferiority, immaturity, lowered social competence and higher incidence of behavior problems, depression and suicidal ideation, and psychiatric disorders.[4]

One of the most consistent findings among adolescents with disabilities is that they have significant difficulties in social development. By the time children with disabilities reach the teen years, they have often had a history of peer rejection, social isolation, and social ineffectiveness.[5] As a result of these significant social deficits, adolescents with chronic disabilities are often socially isolated and disliked by peers; thus they are likely to present to counselors as lonely, anxious, depressed, timid, and lacking in self-confidence.[6]

---

Rich was diagnosed with Tourette's syndrome when he was eleven. By the time he was referred for counseling as part of his school placement at age fifteen, Rich had a history of uncontrollable eye blinking and vocal tics and of touching others inappropriately, lecturing and monopolizing conversations, and shouting in class. He had no friends either in school or at home, tended to withdraw and isolate himself, engaged in impulsive behaviors such as fighting with peers, and had suicidal ideation.

I spent initial sessions establishing trust, by allowing Rich to talk about philosophical ideas that in and of themselves were unrelated to his presenting problems. I also spent a lot of time empathizing with his distrust of others by self-disclosing some of my own fears of looking foolish and feelings of being different at times.

# INTELLECTUALLY GIFTED ADOLESCENTS

The definition of intellectual giftedness has changed over the years, but the term generally refers to those adolescents who score at an extreme (for example, at or above the ninety-eighth percentile) on a standardized intelligence test. Gifted adolescents negotiate the developmental demands of the teen years differently than other young people. Experts have noted, "To have the intellect of an adult and the emotions of a child combined in a childish body is to encounter certain difficulties."[7]

Gifted adolescents often have problems relating to peers. They tend to have little patience for superficiality and are often cynical and argumentative. Thus they often feel socially alienated and uncomfortable in their peer group.[8] This recognition of being different than most other kids results in feelings of inferiority and inadequacy, as these young people can't seem to find their place in the world.

---

Rebecca was thirteen years old when I started seeing her in psychotherapy during her parents' divorce. Even though she was in a class for gifted students, she was clearly superior academically to most of her peers. She was also a talented actress and spent much of her free time performing with a theater company.

Although the initial referral was to help her adjust to the divorce, it was evident to me that many of her problems stemmed from her giftedness; her behaviors highlight how such adolescents often present in treatment.

Rebecca had very high expectations of herself and others; she had little tolerance or patience for peers who asked "stupid" questions in class. She thought nothing of making sarcastic comments out loud in response to these "stupid" questions, often creating a disruption in class. Similarly, she found much of the material in school boring and irrelevant, and delighted in catching her teachers in a mistake. Rebecca told me that she loved getting into arguments with teachers just to show them up, even if these resulted in being sent to the principal's office.

Despite this apparent bravado, Rebecca was devastated when she was not peer-nominated to represent her class at a school debate. She reportedly had a temper tantrum in class, calling the teacher and the other students all kinds of names. She denied feeling hurt, ascribing her emotional outburst to an unfair voting process and bias on the teacher's part.

During the initial session, Rebecca presented as pseudomature. She made it clear that she didn't believe she had any problems, and tried to engage me in an intellectual discussion of the merits of psychotherapy. She responded to many of my comments with sarcasm and changed any topic that was risky for her to discuss. Rebecca acknowledged that she had few friends and that her classmates didn't really like her, but she rationalized that she didn't have much time for socializing, and besides, most of the kids she knew were "too immature" for her.

The topic on which she and I began our therapeutic journey was the theater. She told me the parts she had played and what roles she hoped to play in the future. I shared my own love of the theater from having grown up in New York City and having attended many Broadway shows, and how one of my secret wishes had always been to act in musical comedy. We talked about the differences between stage acting and "real life" and about the depth it took an actor to play a role passionately. Did we talk about her classroom behavior during our first session? Only indirectly, because we were certainly talking about "making a scene" and how sometimes people didn't understand the meaning behind particular verbal phrases or nonverbal movements. We reflected on the fact that many times, actors were misunderstood by the general public, and how people often made assumptions about actors without really knowing them. We may not have talked directly about Rebecca's feeling but we definitely made progress in establishing a working relationship.

# ADOLESCENTS WITH
# LEARNING DISABILITIES

Children with learning disabilities face significant challenges once they reach adolescence. As noted by several researchers, severe deficits in academic, cognitive, social, and emotional functioning are not uncommon.[9]

Teens with learning disabilities may be referred to counselors due to difficulties in academic performance. Problems in mathematics are common in this population, as are difficulties in oral and written language, handwriting, spelling and word usage, and reading.[10] In addition to these content areas, adolescents with learning disabilities frequently show deficits in study skills, test taking, note taking, listening comprehension, attention and concentration, and independent thinking.[11]

Many times, teenagers with learning disabilities are referred for therapy because of the social-emotional behaviors typical of this group. For example, 25 to 40 percent of children with learning disabilities also have attention deficit disorders: attentional problems, hyperactivity, and impulsivity are often present.[12]

A major area of concern for adolescents with learning disabilities is their peer relationships. These teens are unlikely to participate in school or extracurricular activities and may have infrequent and negative interactions with peers.[13] As a result, their social skills are often poor, and they are likely to be dependent on their parents longer than their peers without disabilities. They may present to therapists as isolated and lonely, and feeling relatively powerless to change the situation.

An additional area of concern that therapists need to keep in mind is the increased risk of suicidal ideation in adolescents with learning disabilities.[14] Teens with learning disabilities tend to have a depressive cognitive style, attributing success to external factors and failure to their own inabilities. Continued academic and social failures only confirm their beliefs about their own helplessness, and thoughts about suicide may occur more frequently than in other diagnostic groups.

When we are referred an adolescent having school problems or with a diagnosable learning disability, it is thus always important to inquire about his attributions. What reason does the teenager give himself for these school failures? Does he blame them on stable traits about himself ("I'm such a loser")? Does he believe things will get worse ("I'll continue to fail not only in school but in everything I try")?

As we would with a depressed teen, we should ask directly about suicide and begin immediately to challenge the young person's negative beliefs about herself by discussing the availability of strategies to deal with learning problems. I also tell the teenager about several of my graduate students who, despite severe learning disabilities, went on to achieve their doctorates. By providing such examples and offering the possibility of compensatory strategies, we instill hope in the teen and begin to replace negative cognitions with more optimistic thoughts.

# ADOLESCENTS IN DEVIANT SUBCULTURES

The proliferation of drive-by shootings and attacks on middle school and high school campuses over the past several years has alerted mental health practitioners to the presence of deviant adolescent subcultures, such as those of skinheads and violent street gangs. It's commonly believed that teens who feel alienated from society seek others who provide a sense of identity and belonging for them. They may thus get involved with cults, gangs, or movements that confirm their self-worth and offer a sense of "family" to them.

How do these young people look compared to most teens? Many seem depressed: they have a cynical, pessimistic view of life and seem to lack humor and spontaneity. Suicidal ideation and gestures are common, as are such symptoms as hopelessness and withdrawal.

It is also not uncommon to find an increase in acting-out behaviors, such as drug and alcohol abuse, truancy, acts of aggression, sexual promiscuity or interest in pornography, cruelty to animals, and family conflicts. We also see changes in habits, such as the teen's choice of friends or clothing, or listening to music or watching movies that glorify violence.

In engaging with such teens, it's important to be familiar with the language and practices of the subculture, just as one would be expected to understand any minority culture. Don't expect the adolescent to reveal too much early in treatment; secretiveness is often part of the membership criteria in the gang or cult, so the young person will not be ready to give this up. Similarly, we need to respect the fact that giving up association with the subculture is like asking the adolescent to give up who he is—until he has something to replace it with, he'll hang onto it. Instead, I talk to the teen about the group itself—when and how he got involved and what it's like to belong. I also talk to the young person about reality issues, such as fears for his life and the lives of his friends and family. I slowly move into more psychological issues, such as self-esteem and family problems, but not until the teen feels my interest and respect.

---

I once had an initial appointment with a single-parent mother and her fourteen-year-old daughter, Vanessa. Mom had been referred to therapy because Vanessa's grades had slipped considerably, and her teachers had noticed her falling asleep in class and being distracted of late.

When I turned the corner to my waiting room, I was caught by surprise. Vanessa was tall and thin and dressed completely in black, with black lipstick, black nail polish, and black-accented eyebrows and eyelashes. After I caught my breath, I invited both mom and

Vanessa into my office. Mom detailed her concerns while Vanessa sat quietly; neither one mentioned the teen's appearance.

I asked mom to leave, and rather than talk about the presenting problem, I said to Vanessa, "I'm fascinated by your outfit. Tell me about it." After some hesitation, Vanessa described for me when and how she started to dress that way. I stayed away from asking her what statement she was trying to make, but knowing that adolescents in deviant subcultures often feel lost and depressed, I said, "I'll bet it's sometimes hard to connect with the other kids at school." Vanessa then talked about not feeling like she fit in and feeling like even her mom didn't understand her.

It became readily apparent to me that beneath her dramatic exterior, Vanessa was a scared, lonely girl. Like other teens who try to be accepted, Vanessa's style of dress and interaction only produced more isolation. The focus of much of our therapeutic work became how Vanessa could connect with others, including her mother, without having to compromise her integrity.

# ADOLESCENTS IN DIVORCING FAMILIES

Numerous studies have examined the relationship between divorce and the adjustment of children and adolescents. Although teens can understand divorce more abstractly than can younger children, they must also deal with the painful feelings of the family disruption at the same time as they are struggling to define their own identity. As a result, adolescents whose parents divorce are likely to be at greater risk for psychosocial difficulties than are their peers in two-parent families. For example, adolescents from divorced homes show higher rates of school problems and dropout, substance abuse, early sexuality, emotional problems, and delinquency. These problems typically result from the adverse effects of economic and other life changes on a parent's ability to be effective with her children.

Adolescents from divorced homes may thus seem out of control. Single parents, feeling overwhelmed themselves, often lose perspective on what's normal and respond to their adolescent with excessive punishment or verbal abuse, exacerbating the young person's alienation from the family. Normal testing of limits may become serious rule violations, as parents no longer have time or patience to monitor their teen's behavior, and conduct problems and delinquency may result.

In addition to delinquency, adolescents from divorced families may be referred for school failures or truancy. These young people may have moved into new neighborhoods after the divorce and therefore lack peer and community supports in addition to having lost effective parenting. One way I understand and frame a teen's behavior following divorce is that it is a reminder to her parent that she still needs a sense of family, and needs guidance and direction from the parent.

Some teens feel the loss of the family directly and become depressed and sometimes suicidal. They may feel caught in a loyalty bind between the parents and feel as though they can't talk to either parent about their sadness over the marital breakup. They grieve not only the actual loss of the family but also the change in lifestyle, finances, and sense of predictability they once had.

In meeting with adolescents whose parents are divorced, I always assess how the divorce has affected the parents, for two major reasons. One, the custodial parent may be grieving herself, may feel intense anger at the ex-spouse, and may feel helpless about the future. The teen's moods and behavior might be the teen's way of protecting the parent from these painful feelings—as long as the child has the symptoms, the parent can mobilize to help the teen and not have to think about her own anguish. Second, because the major predictor of child adjustment after divorce is the conflict between the ex-spouses, it's important for us to assess the level of conflict and work toward removing the adolescent from being in the middle of the unresolved conflict.

# ADOLESCENTS IN STEPFAMILIES

Considering the high rates of divorce and remarriage in the United States, many of the adolescents we are likely to see will be part of a stepfamily. The complex issues of forming a stepfamily interact with the normal developmental tasks of adolescence to create an increased risk of psychosocial, learning, and health-related problems in teens who are in stepfamilies.[15] At the time of the remarriage, many adolescents show a reemergence of behavior problems from childhood that are related to unresolved issues between the ex-partners.[16] Other research has found that forming a remarried family when a child is in early adolescence may result in teenagers showing increased levels of conduct problems and acting-out behaviors.[17]

Experts note six major issues for adolescents in stepfamilies: (1) developmental issues, (2) sexuality, (3) parent-child relationships, (4) parenting, (5) nonresidential parent-child issues, and (6) changes in visitation and custody.[18] Each of these issues may be related to the problems presented by teens and their families during initial counseling sessions. For example, in the early stages of stepfamily development, the new spouses are trying to establish a cohesive family unit, whereas the adolescent in this family is pulling away and trying to establish an independent life apart from the family.

---

I once worked with a newly married couple and the woman's fourteen-year-old daughter from her first marriage, Becky. The adults' agenda was to convince the girl that because they had very few possible years together as a family unit, Becky should spend most of every weekend with them, doing "family" activities. The young teen had a different goal: for the adults to allow her to spend time with her friends at the mall!

Not only was this mom having a tough time letting her daughter grow up, but she was now getting support from her new husband, who had never had any kids and wanted the sense of "family," for keeping the teenager from establishing age-appropriate autonomy. A classic conflict of life-cycle demands!

Becky clearly did not want to be in therapy. She felt blamed by her mom for not being cooperative with the family and was considering moving to her dad's house. She approached me with distrust: Was I going to agree with her mom and tell her she needed to comply with mom's demands? I knew that if Becky didn't immediately sense my support, she'd be highly resistant to returning for a second session, and I'd be playing into the family dynamic of mom insisting on compliance.

"Sounds to me like a compromise is needed," I said. Becky's ears perked up as I discussed how Becky's developmental needs were to pull away and begin to establish a life of her own, whereas her mom and stepfather's need was to gain a sense of "family." We talked about how they could each gain a little of what they wanted while respecting the other's needs, and they decided, for a start, that Becky could spend Friday evenings and overnights with her friends in exchange for Sunday afternoon outings as a whole family.

---

Because of their own burgeoning sexuality, adolescents in stepfamilies may also be particularly sensitive to signs of intimacy between the two spouses. As well, expressions of affection from a stepparent to a stepteen may feel threatening to the teen, and the discomfort may interfere with bonding between the adolescent and stepparent. We need to be alert to these issues, because the discomfort experienced by the teen may be a realistic reaction to an adult who is acting inappropriately. Because there are more reports of stepfather-stepdaughter molestations than biological father-daughter reports we must thoroughly evaluate a stepdaughter's discomfort to make sure that her personal boundaries aren't being violated. Although reports of sexual abuse of male stepteens are scant in number, we must always be alert to signs of such boundary violations in the population as well.

Relationships in stepfamilies are constantly being tested. Whereas biological parents may understand their child's moods from living with him all their lives, stepparents may take the teen's obnoxious behaviors personally.[19] Both the stepparent and custodial parent may insist that the teenager love and respect the new adult, who may have taken on an inappropriate parenting role, resulting in huge power struggles and loyalty conflicts. I've had numerous referrals of adolescents in stepfamilies where the presenting issues boiled down to, "I'm going to lose my new spouse if my teenager doesn't shape up." Once again, educating such families and helping them clarify their roles help enormously.

An example of a stepparent taking on an inappropriate role is a new stepfather who enters the system as the disciplinarian. Whether the stepfather himself insists on playing this role, or the mother invites him to do so when she feels powerless, the stepfather's being such a high-profile figure is highly disruptive to the new family unit. It is important for us to discuss with the new spouses that the biological parent should be the primary disciplinarian for a while so as to allow the stepparent to concentrate on nurturing his relationship with the stepkids, much like a friend or baby-sitter.

# MINORITY ADOLESCENTS

Over the next twenty years the demographics of adolescents in the United States will change dramatically. By the year 2020, the majority of school-age children in the United States will be members of ethnic minority groups.[20] Because of these changes, we need to gain awareness and skills to provide effective culturally responsive counseling.

For many minority adolescents, fitting in has meant that they have had to reject parts of their heritage. Doing so may result in their feeling different from both their own culture as well as that of the majority, and they may present with symptoms of loneliness, self-hate, anger, and depression.[21] They may experience rejection from other teens in the majority culture as well as be criticized by their parents for being "too American." In the process of identity development, then, adolescents from other cultures sometimes don't know which way to turn.

Many minority adolescents are fairly acculturated, so they present very much like American teenagers. They may display remnants of behaviors and attitudes specific to their culture, however, and we certainly must be familiar with cultural norms and practices to do effective work with these teens. Because the young person's understanding of the world comes, in large part, from family members who may have immigrated from elsewhere, our ability to respond empathically includes being able to understand the teen from a cultural perspective.

Doing effective work with minority teens means that before you begin working with a teen from a different culture, you would be wise to educate yourself about cultural differences. Pushing a teen in a direction consistent with American values (for example, "express your feelings") may result in a loss of your credibility if the behavior is incongruent with that of the client's culture, even if the young person seems very acculturated. With most minority teens, what helps is for you to empathize with the pressures and struggles the teen experiences by being caught between the two cultures.

Showing we care and can be trusted also means acting in ways that demonstrate a respect for the minority adolescent's culture. For example, asking an Asian teen about physical symptoms, discussing practical matters rather than feelings with Native American teens, and self-disclosing to African American adolescents convey an acceptance and acknowledgment of the young person's heritage.[22]

I've also found it particularly helpful to involve the adolescent's family, sometimes even the extended family, early in the process, because principles of collectivism and connectedness are typically strong in most minority cultures. Educating the family about the process of counseling and how it will help the teen goes a long way toward engaging everyone and preventing premature termination.

I also have found it very useful to discuss with adolescents and their
families the importance of ethnicity to their lives, as family conflicts often arise when children begin to develop a lifestyle that is
different from that of their parents.

Experts in the field of culturally responsive counseling suggest
several considerations in developing effective therapeutic relationships with minority adolescents; I have summarized these considerations in the list that follows.[23]

- Minority teens and their families may have had a history of frustrating relationships with authority figures in
  the past and may thus be mistrusting of therapists. Such
  clients may therefore test your knowledge of their culture as well as how much you really care about them.

- Adolescents from different cultures must feel that you
  accept their belief system and care about them as wor-
  thy of respect. This means that counselors whose culture or ethnicity is different than that of the teen
  should bring up the issue of "differentness," in terms of
  how the teen experiences her differentness from her
  peers as well as how the young client feels about working with a therapist from a different background.

- Because clients from other cultures expect improvement to occur soon, you should communicate to teens
  and their families that at least a partial relief from
  symptoms is possible within a relatively short period
  of time.

- Structuring the session and explaining to the clients
  the purpose of various questions and interventions are
  important to your gaining clients' trust.

- A treatment style that is active and directive works
  better than a detached, reflective style.

- Be prepared to use a multidimensional approach, including referrals to medical, spiritual, and community resources, and to incorporate extended family members into the treatment.

- Attend to real-world issues as well as more psychological ones—that is, give practical advice and talk about what's important to the minority teen instead of focusing too much on feelings or underlying process issues.

In sum, you need to prepare for work with adolescent clients from diverse backgrounds by both examining your own biases and stereotypes and educating yourself about the cultural group of the specific teenager. An approach that is active and practical, that includes other resources, and that incorporates the family's heritage and belief system is most likely to produce positive outcomes for the young client.

---

Although adolescents from special populations have the same fundamental needs as all teenagers, your engagement with these teens is definitely facilitated by your knowledge of that population and your ability to convey your understanding empathically. As stated throughout this book, your task in the first session is to establish a working relationship with the adolescent. Given that teens won't necessarily connect their symptoms with their cultural background, disability, or family environment, you must be able to make these connections so that you understand the young person's behavior in context; in later sessions you might find it therapeutic to help the teen understand these connections by making them explicit. By taking these dynamics into account, you will behave in the first session in ways that maintain your credibility and gain the client's trust, which will set the stage for the remainder of the treatment.

In Chapter Seven I'll present a case study of an adolescent and his family in order to illustrate how the material I've discussed may be applied to a real case.

# 7

# Case Study: Jeremy

In this final chapter, we'll use the case of an adolescent with whom I worked in the recent past as a way of bringing to life some of the strategies I detailed in the preceding chapters. As you read this, note that the focus is on engagement in the first session, not on doing a differential diagnosis or on long-term treatment planning.

## PRESENTING PROBLEM

Jeremy was a fifteen-year-old boy with a younger sister, Holly, age twelve. He lived part-time with his mother (Leslie) and part-time with his father (Michael Stein) and stepmother (Susan). Michael, a pharmacist, called me with concerns about Jeremy's attitude and moods. He described that over the course of the past six to nine months, Jeremy had become increasingly withdrawn and isolated, often staying in his room except for meals. He would eat dinner very quickly and typically in silence.

Of greater concern to dad was that Jeremy wouldn't even say hello to his stepmother, and responded to even the mildest of dad's comments with anger and, sometimes, tears. Michael noted that Jeremy was talking about going to live with his mother full-time, which, according to dad, was out of the question. Michael was concerned that Jeremy was depressed; he attributed Jeremy's actions and desire to live with his mother to the depression. Being a pharmacist, he wondered if his son needed antidepressant medication.

## RELEVANT HISTORY

Jeremy and Holly had lived with both biological parents until four years ago, when Michael and Leslie separated. The divorce was relatively amicable, and mom and dad worked out a joint physical custody arrangement whereby the children lived with each parent one week at a time.

Jeremy was an excellent student and a talented pianist. He got along well with his peers, though he tended to be a bit distant and had no "best" friend. Jeremy was not interested in participatory sports, but he enjoyed watching a ball game on TV or at the stadium with his father. When with his mother, he enjoyed shopping, movies, and restaurants.

Prior to the marital separation, Jeremy's life was unremarkable. Dad worked a lot, and mom raised the children in addition to pursuing her career as a legal assistant. The parents grew distant over the years and divorced when it was discovered that dad was seeing a younger woman (currently thirty), whom he married two years ago. Stepmom had never been married, had no children, and was of a different ethnic background and religion. Jeremy and his family were practicing Jews who lived all their lives in a major city, whereas Susan grew up in a small midwestern town and was Catholic.

## THE INITIAL PHONE CALL

Michael called me after a major argument with Jeremy concerning the way he was allegedly treating his stepmother. He told me that Jeremy broke into tears, accused his father of not caring about him, and said he wanted to live with his mother.

In order for me to gauge the importance of scheduling an immediate appointment, I asked Michael if he had a concern about suicide. He replied that he didn't think Jeremy was suicidal but that his son had been so moody lately that he didn't know what to expect. I told him it would be wise to err on the cautious side and to be sure that someone would be around Jeremy (that is, at home) at all times until we could meet.

I inquired about who else lived at home, and was told that stepmom and sister resided there along with dad and Jeremy. "I'd like to set an appointment for as soon as possible, and I'd like for all four of you to be present," I told him. He asked, "Why do Susan and Holly have to come?"

I responded that it was helpful to my work to meet the entire family and get everyone's perspective. "I don't plan to have everyone attend all future sessions," I reassured him, "but I'd like the family there for the first session so that everyone can give me their ideas about what's going on and in what ways I can be helpful to everyone."

I then asked if Jeremy's biological mom knew what was going on. Michael said he had been discussing his concerns about their son with his ex-wife all along. He added that he thought she was part of the problem, however, as she was supposedly telling Jeremy that if he continued to have problems at his dad's house, he could live with her full-time. I told Michael that after our first meeting, I would need to call Leslie and get her consent to work with Jeremy, and that I would likely invite her in for a session with Jeremy as well.

Dad asked what he should say to Jeremy about meeting with me. I advised him to be honest with his son and to tell him that he (dad) was very worried about him and felt like he (dad) needed some help concerning how best to handle the conflict in the home. I suggested he tell Jeremy that he had called me and that I had scheduled an appointment for everyone in the household to come in so that I could get everyone's ideas about what was going on. "If Jeremy complains that he doesn't need to see a shrink, tell him that's why I want everyone to come in—so that I can consult with all of you, and together we can figure out how to improve the situation." Dad agreed to bring Susan and Holly along with Jeremy, and we set up the appointment for the next afternoon.

## THE FIRST FAMILY SESSION

Just prior to meeting the family, my receptionist had Michael and his wife sign the Informed Consent to Treatment agreement and had dad sign the Consent to Treat Minors form. Jeremy and Holly were asked to read and sign an Assent to Treatment form.

When I met the family in the waiting room, I said, "Hi, I'm Dr. Ribner," and shook Michael's and Susan's hands as they introduced themselves. I walked over to Jeremy, again said, "I'm Dr. Ribner," and reached out my hand. He silently and reluctantly shook my hand, and I said, "You're . . . ?"

"Jeremy," he muttered under his breath.

"Hi, Jeremy, nice to meet you," I replied. I then moved over to Holly, who smiled, took my hand, and said, "Holly." As she was wearing a Mia Hamm T-shirt, I asked, "Do you play soccer?" When she acknowledged that she did, I remarked that "all my kids have played—and I coached their teams when they were your age." I then asked the family to come into my office.

Dad and Susan sat together on one couch, and Jeremy and Holly sat on opposite ends of another couch. "Thanks for reading these forms," I said. "Does anyone have any questions about them?" Seeing that they didn't, I said, "Let me get to know each of you a little bit." Because I wanted the adolescent to feel respected and that I wasn't aligning with the adults, I turned to him and said, "Jeremy, why don't you start. Tell me a little about yourself, like what you've been doing this summer."

After a painful minute of silence, he said, "I'll pass."

Michael interrupted to tell his son to answer the question, but I said, "That's fine. We can come back to you later if you'd like."

"Holly, I know you like soccer; tell me about it." She described her team, and I showed sincere interest by asking follow-up questions and remarking, "That's great! I'll bet the team really counts on you" when she told me that she had scored two goals in a game last week. I then asked Michael and Susan to tell me a little about their lives as well. When they finished, I asked Jeremy again if he wanted to share anything about his life, and he shook his head no and continued to look at the ground.

"I wanted all of you here because usually when there's a problem in a family, people have different ideas about what the problem really is. So, today I'd like to hear from everyone as to what you think the family is struggling with, and how you think I can be helpful. Who would like to start?"

After a short period of silence, Michael said, "We're here because we're concerned about Jeremy's behavior recently."

I wanted to set a rule about each person talking for himself or herself, so I said to Michael, "Say more, but tell me about *your* concerns, and then I'll find out from the others about their concerns." He went on to describe how for the past several months, Jeremy had gotten more reclusive, hardly emerging from his room. Dad added that Jeremy had been rude and disrespectful to his stepmother as well.

I asked Michael to say how Jeremy showed rudeness and disrespect, and he detailed that what bothered him the most was that Jeremy would often walk by Susan and not even acknowledge her presence. Wanting to begin defining the problem in interpersonal terms, I then asked Michael how he reacted when Jeremy behaved that way. "I try to talk to him, but we wind up arguing, and Jeremy goes off to his room and slams the door."

In order to understand how dad framed the problem, I asked him, "What's your best sense of how your concern for your son turns into an argument, Michael?"

Dad stated, "I guess we don't communicate that well—I always thought we did, but now I don't know."

To begin the process of reframing in interpersonal terms, I said, "So you're having difficulty communicating your worry to Jeremy in a way that reaches him." I noticed that Jeremy picked up his head slightly and looked at his dad.

"I guess so," replied Michael.

In an educative tone, I responded, "As kids get older, sometimes we have to change our style of communicating with them—I had to learn the same lesson with my own children."

I did not want the session to turn into a forum for dad blaming the teenager, so I moved on and asked Susan what she felt was going on. She was more critical than Michael, insisting that she had tried her best to get along with Jeremy but that he wasn't even pleasant with her, much less respectful. "I've never been a mother before," she said, "but in my family a child would never treat an adult like Jeremy treats me." I asked her to elaborate, and she said, "When I pick him up from school, he gets in the car and doesn't even say hello. I ask him how his day was, and he acts like he's deaf. I'm not his chauffeur. If I go out of my way to do something for him, like give him a ride, the least he can do is say thank you."

In an attempt to take some of the sting away from her comments, I asked Susan if there were any exceptions to the unpleasantness— that is, times that she and Jeremy got along well. Susan reluctantly admitted that occasionally they had some relatively neutral times, though she attributed this to Jeremy's wanting something, such as a ride to the library.

I tried to normalize and lighten the situation by interjecting that "there seems to be something in what we're feeding teenagers nowadays, since they all seem to be like that."

Interestingly, Michael then supported his son, saying, "It's not just nowadays—I was like that when I was a kid also."

In response to my next question, Susan denied that there were any other problems in the family, claiming to get along perfectly well with Michael and Holly, though she did say that sometimes Michael's ex-wife, Leslie, created some problems.

I chose not to go into this topic, setting a boundary between adult issues and those that the children should be talking about. Instead, I asked Holly for her impressions of the situation. As often happens in families when one member is attacked, Holly defended her brother, acknowledging that sometimes Jeremy and Susan didn't get along but adding that she thought Susan didn't understand Jeremy. Specifically, she said that Susan didn't understand how Jeremy felt about her religion or about how things used to be before she moved in.

Seeing this as an opportunity to engage Jeremy, I turned to him. "Is what Holly said correct, Jeremy? That there are some things you feel Susan doesn't understand about you?"

Looking down, he responded, "I guess." He immediately looked at his father and said, "Dad, I have a lot of homework. How much longer are we gonna be here?"

Michael answered, "Jeremy, I told you this is important. We'll be here until the doctor tells us we can go."

Sensing this as a set-up for me to be the bad guy, which would create distrust for the teen, I jumped in. "I'm sure there are many more places you'd rather be than in a therapist's office, Jeremy. We're scheduled for about ten more minutes today. There are still some things that are puzzling me about the family, and I haven't heard yet what you think everyone is struggling with. What do you think about what's been said so far?"

Jeremy rolled his eyes and said, "I don't care what they think. All I know is I have a lot of homework. It's the beginning of school, and I can't afford to fall behind."

"I promise we'll wrap up in ten minutes," I said. "But before we stop, I'd like to give you a chance to say what you'd like to see changed in the family."

"You keep calling this a family," he said. "This isn't my family; my family is my mother and father and sister."

"My apologies; that was insensitive of me," I responded.

Jeremy then said, "I just want them to leave me alone."

Although my assessment of this statement was that Jeremy really wanted the opposite—that is, for dad to give him more attention and nurturance—I did not challenge the adolescent's statement. When Michael started to confront Jeremy, however, I made a quick decision so that I could try to connect with the teen before the session was over. "Let's do this," I said to dad. "Why don't you and Susan and Holly go out to the waiting room and give me a few minutes alone with Jeremy."

After they left, I said to Jeremy, "It must be hard to feel like you can't even be honest and say what you want without someone jumping down your throat."

"Yeah, well ever since Susan's been around, my dad always takes her side. And he's changed so much, I don't even know him anymore."

I didn't want to ask an open-ended question about how he felt; as this was the first session, I did not want him to think I was being too intrusive. Instead I commented, "You must feel like you don't even have a family any more."

Jeremy answered, "My mother said I could come live with her if I want to, but my dad doesn't want me to."

As before, I didn't want to ask him too many trite, "How do you feel about that?" questions, so I commented, "And you're feeling pretty discouraged about the whole situation." Jeremy didn't respond. I added, "No wonder you sometimes don't want to be around your dad and Susan. Your room must feel like the only safe place in the house."

"It's not even like my dad's such a bad guy," Jeremy said. "He just gets weird when Susan's around."

The session was almost over. My main goals at this point were for Jeremy to feel that I could be helpful to him and for him to be willing to return for another session. I said, "So you and your dad had a good relationship for many years."

"So?" he responded.

"I'd like to see if you and I can figure out some ways for you two to reconnect. I know that might seem impossible right now, but I hate thinking that the only option you've found is to be depressed and alone in your own house."

I decided to briefly educate Jeremy about treatment. "I meet a lot with teenagers and families and help them work out their conflicts. Most of the time, the kids feel pretty discouraged, and I usually find it helpful to get to know the teenager first. Then, because you know your family much better than I ever will, I'll get your thoughts on how we can try to get through to them. Are you open to giving it a shot?" There was a slight head nod, but no words, from Jeremy.

I added that "I'm also concerned about how depressed you are, so I want to ask you a few quick questions before we end today." I asked Jeremy about his eating and sleeping recently, about any suicidal thoughts he had, whether or not he had a suicide plan, and whom he would call if he felt overwhelmed. He said he was going to spend the next week with his mother, where he didn't feel nearly as depressed as he did at his dad's.

Judging his suicide risk to be mild, I said, "How about if you and I meet next week when you get back to your dad's house, and we can get to know each other a little and see what we can work out?" Jeremy agreed to meet with me but wanted to know what I'd tell his father. I reviewed the rules about confidentiality and mandatory reporting, and told him I'd also need to get his mother's consent to work with him.

I then invited the others back in, told them Jeremy and I were going to meet alone for the next session, and reviewed confidentiality with them as well. I also told Michael that I'd be calling Jeremy's mother to let her know I'd be meeting with him and to get her consent, and would likely have a session with her and Jeremy in the future.

Michael asked me if I thought Jeremy needed medication. After clarifying for him that, as a psychologist, I could not make medical decisions, I asked him to let me get to know Jeremy a bit better before I decided whether or not to refer him for a psychiatric consult. I then gave Jeremy an appointment card and told him that he could call me at any time and that I'd get back to him usually within an hour.

## CALLING THE OTHER PARENT

After this session, I called Leslie to let her know that Michael had brought Jeremy in to see me and that I was calling her to see how she felt about her son being in treatment. She indicated her support and volunteered to be available to come in for a session and to help in any way she could. I told her I would likely have a meeting with her and Jeremy in a couple of weeks and might even have her come in for a session with Jeremy and Michael if the situation called for it. I then faxed her the Consent to Treat Minors form for her signature.

## THE FIRST SESSION
## WITH THE ADOLESCENT ALONE

When the time came for the first appointment with Jeremy, I walked to the waiting room and found him and his dad sitting as far away from each other as they could. Before I could say anything, Michael asked if he could talk with me for a few minutes before I met with his son. "If it's something concerning Jeremy," I said, "I'd prefer that we all go to my office, and you can tell me in front of him what you'd like me to know. That way, I'm not translating things you think are important."

When we got to my office and sat down, I tried to find a common ground. "You both look so unhappy," I said. Jeremy was silent and looked away.

Michael said, "Jeremy just got back from his mom's last night, and he and Susan already had an incident." He went on to say that Susan picked the kids up from school today, and Jeremy didn't say hello or even acknowledge her. According to Michael, Susan told Jeremy that she was tired of doing all the work to try to have a good relationship with him, and he told her she could just leave if she didn't like it. At the next stop light, Jeremy exited the car and walked home.

In order to understand the sequence of family interactions, I asked Michael how he found out what had happened. He related that Susan called him at work, and he left early and came home, only to find Susan upset and Jeremy alone in his room. He said he tried to talk to his son, who cried and would only say how miserable he was and that he wanted to go live with his mom. Michael then tried to calm Susan down, but felt terribly torn between his wife and his child. To his credit, he expressed concern about the level of Jeremy's depression, though he was mostly attentive to what he described as the teen's "ungrateful attitude" and "unwillingness to compromise."

I asked Michael to wait in the waiting room while I spoke to Jeremy alone. As soon as his father left, Jeremy said, "This sucks! I shouldn't have to be here—he should."

I acknowledged how awful it must be to live around all that tension and said, "My sense is that everyone in the family has some things to learn."

"Then how come you're meeting with me and not them?" he asked.

I answered, "Because I'm worried about you. Your dad has Susan for support, but I'm worried that you feel all alone in this family. And like we talked about last week, I'd like to see if I can help you figure out some ways to reconnect with your dad." Jeremy was silent and looking down, but he was listening. "Once I get to know you a little better, and we go over some strategies, we'll have your dad and maybe Susan join us so I can help you negotiate some changes in the house."

"I'm not coming if Susan comes," Jeremy adamantly stated.

"Let's not worry about that now," I answered. "The main problem seems to be between you and your dad anyway. And I'll never bring someone in without discussing it with you first. Are you OK with meeting with me a couple of times—just you and me?"

"What are we gonna talk about?" he asked.

"Let's start by having you tell me what happened this afternoon when Susan picked you up," I answered.

"It's not like she said," Jeremy noted. "I did say hi but she doesn't hear me. She expects us to be all happy when we see her. And then she goes and calls my dad, and he always takes her side. He's always telling me I should compromise and that Susan is trying her best to have a happy family. I never hear him tell her that *she* needs to compromise. And who wants her in our family anyway?"

I felt like empathizing with the depth of Jeremy's despair, but I didn't want to frighten him by putting him in touch with deep feelings right away. Instead I chose to ask about attempted solutions. "What have you tried so far to get your father to listen to you?"

"He won't," the adolescent replied. "Every time I tell him about something Susan did, he tells me it's not that way and that I need to understand that she's trying her best."

Again, I chose not to pursue the intensity of this experience for him, given that it was our first session together. "Does Holly get into trouble with your dad?" I asked.

"They think she's so perfect," Jeremy replied. "But she tells me how she hates Susan also."

Wanting to underscore any support Jeremy might have had in the family, I said, "So you and Holly talk about it sometimes?"

"A little bit," he answered. "But Susan spoils her and takes her shopping, so she won't say anything to my dad."

I asked if there was anyone else Jeremy talked to. He said his mom knew what was going on, and he again stated that Leslie had told him he could live with her. I didn't see this as a viable solution because Michael had made it very clear that he was not about to give up custody, but I didn't want to challenge Jeremy so early into our work. Instead I commented that "regardless of where you live, Jeremy, you and your dad need to work this out."

The tension in the room had dissipated considerably. Although it was obvious to me that Jeremy was acting in ways that elicited his stepmother's disapproval and his father's pleadings, the first session was not the time to confront or challenge him. I was much more interested in engaging him in the process and having him leave the session knowing I was genuinely interested in him and could advocate for him. I decided, then, to put the problem focus aside and to talk about Jeremy's life. I hoped that this would help us connect and allow Jeremy to see that I wanted to get to know *him*, not just his problem. As a segue, I asked, "What did you enjoy doing with your dad before Susan came onto the scene?"

"We used to go to ball games or watch TV or go to movies a lot," he answered.

"Do you still enjoy those activities?" I asked.

"A little bit," he responded. "I'm pretty busy with school and homework and piano lessons."

"You play piano?" I enthusiastically responded. "I'm jealous—I love music, but playing an instrument has always been like learning a foreign language to me. What type of music do you play?" Jeremy went on to describe his interests and musical style. I told him of some of my favorite memories of hearing chamber music played in small churches in Europe, and this sparked a discussion of places he wanted to visit.

"Your days sound as busy as mine," I commented. "Do you have any time for friends?" Jeremy described having had a couple of good friends through grade school but not having anyone he felt very close to recently. I disclosed about a time in my adolescence when my interests were changing, and I was getting more serious about my schoolwork and felt I no longer had much in common with some of my old friends.

"That's the same with me," he remarked. "It's like when I see them, I have nothing to say."

Jeremy asked me what I did about it. I didn't want to give him the impression that I had the answer, yet I wanted him to know it was not that unusual for teens to go through periods of feeling different than their peers. I also wanted to validate his struggle. "I guess I was like you in some ways," I said. "I thought I'd never find friends again. And when I talk to other teenagers nowadays, they tell me they sometimes think the same thing. I remember taking a computer class, and there was a guy in there I knew from other classes. We just started goofing around and then hanging out together."

Noting Jeremy's silence, I added, "But I was surprised when we became friends because it sure felt sometimes like there was no one I could relate to." I continued, "What do you do when you're in your room all evening, Jeremy?"

"Oh, I do homework, or watch TV, or write poems."

"You write poems, too? Gee, I'm with a multitalented kid! Maybe you should be in the therapist's chair asking *me* questions!" He smiled but didn't say anything. "Will you bring me some of your poems to look at?" I asked.

"Maybe," he said. "I'm not very good."

"Well, I'm not very good at judging poetry, so that makes us even," I answered.

As the session was coming to a close, I wanted to begin structuring future sessions. Because I didn't want Jeremy to get too discouraged if he got into an argument with Susan or his father the next week, I asked him if he could predict any situations that might be coming up that I could help him figure out. He said that his dad wanted him to spend winter vacation with him (dad), Holly, and Susan, visiting Susan's family in Minnesota, and he wanted to stay in California with his mom.

I asked if this had to be decided immediately, and Jeremy said he didn't think so (it was only September) but that his dad kept bugging him about it. I responded that this was a good example of the type of issue I could help him negotiate with his dad, and I asked Jeremy if he would mind my asking Michael not to bug him for an answer for a couple of weeks, until we'd had a chance to discuss it in therapy. Jeremy had no problem giving me permission to talk to his dad about this.

When he said he couldn't think of anything else that might create a problem in the upcoming week, I reminded him that often it was the everyday things, like not saying hello, that seemed to be a problem. Wanting to present myself as an advocate, I told Jeremy that with his permission, I would ask his dad not to make a big deal of these things this week and for Michael to ask Susan to do the same.

I then asked Jeremy what he thought he might do, just temporarily, to show his dad that he was trying to work things out and to reassure dad that he didn't have to worry about Jeremy's depression.

"I guess I could say hello to Susan loud enough so that I'm sure she hears me. And I guess I could practice my piano some, instead of staying in my room all night," he responded.

"Both great ideas," I said. "But you know what? When families are trying to make changes, the first few weeks are the hardest, because they're used to doing things in a particular way. So it wouldn't surprise me if you forgot to do one of those things, even though you seem really motivated. It also wouldn't surprise me if Susan or your dad wasn't able to stay out of your way, or if they made it difficult for you, even though they also may want to change. So if it happens that you get into the usual kinds of arguments, will you make some notes about what exactly happened, so we can talk about these next time? Also, I want you to remember that you can call me before we meet next week if you need to talk." Jeremy agreed, and I invited his dad back into the room.

## ENDING THE FIRST SESSION

After Michael returned to the room, I explained that Jeremy and I were going to meet alone again for a time or two and that I would most likely have a conjoint session with Jeremy and him (dad) and one with Jeremy and Leslie after that. I also told Michael that I find it best if the parent doesn't push the teen to talk about what happened in therapy and that he should allow his son to reveal things about the therapy at his own discretion.

In line with what Jeremy and I had talked about, I mentioned that Jeremy had told me about their conflict about going to visit Susan's family in December. I asked dad if he could back off from pressuring Jeremy about this until Jeremy and I had a chance to talk about it, and I promised we would talk to dad in enough time for him to make reservations. He readily agreed.

The last things I mentioned were similar to what I had discussed with Jeremy. I told Michael that because change takes time, it would be best if he and Susan could refrain from being too critical of Jeremy in the upcoming week. I assured him that Jeremy was as interested as he was in trying to resolve the family issues, but that the best way Michael could help Jeremy now was to give him some space and allow him and me to figure things out. I also warned Michael that I wouldn't be surprised if things didn't go very smoothly, even though people were motivated to change, and so not to get too discouraged if the family had an episode of conflict—this was normal.

## OUTCOME OF THE TREATMENT

Jeremy took me up on my offer for him to call me during the week. As was predicted, he and Susan had a run-in, but with my support, Jeremy was able not to get discouraged. Although he presented the incident as a crisis, I understood his calling me as his way of testing whether I would really be there for him. After all, he had experienced his dad repeatedly telling him he could talk to him (dad) any time he needed to, only to be disappointed when Michael took Susan's side. My willingness to speak with him and support him went a long way in securing our connection.

Over the next few sessions, he and I identified several specific issues that needed to get resolved, such as how the stepfamily was going to decorate the house for the holidays (given that they now had different religious preferences) and where Jeremy was going to spend his school vacation. We also dealt with more psychological issues, such as Jeremy feeling left out of the family and wanting to establish a closer relationship with his dad yet not compromising his developmental need for autonomy. I also helped his mother understand how she needed to support her son's working out issues with his dad instead of volunteering to rescue him if things got bad at Michael's house.

Jeremy's depression lifted after approximately five sessions, without any medication. We met for a total of twelve sessions, and a six-month follow-up showed Jeremy to be in good spirits, doing well in school, and developing friendships. Michael was still unhappy with the adolescent's behavior at times, but was no longer worried about the possibility of suicide. Overall, I felt that Jeremy was behaving like a normal teenager!

# Afterword

A colleague of mine once told me that when she advises parents of teens on how to get their child to cooperate, she tells them that there are really two ways of getting chores done: do it yourself or tell the adolescent *not* to do it. The ultimate wisdom in this advice is that interacting with adolescents is not the same as doing so with children or adults, and parents would be well advised to know how best to communicate with their child and know what to expect before trying to engage with them.

As I tried to show in this book, the same wisdom holds for therapists. Understanding teenagers, knowing what to expect, and being prepared to expertly establish connections with adolescents are critical factors in our therapeutic work with young people.

Most courses and books on psychotherapy teach us how to assess, diagnose, and devise treatment plans. Some of these educational materials even present the counseling of the adolescent from a particular theoretical viewpoint, reviewing intervention skills and techniques the authors believe all therapists should learn. And these skills are certainly important! Yet all the diagnostic and therapeutic skills in the world won't go very far if the teen doesn't show up for sessions or lets our words pass in one ear and out the other.

This book was designed to give you suggestions for enhancing the likelihood that the adolescent will return for future sessions and will experience a connection with you so that what you say and do has some impact on their lives. And because every hour you spend with teenage clients is also an hour in your own life, you too can learn and grow from these connections.

So are you ready to go out there and work with adolescents? It's a challenging task, but one that can be incredibly rewarding—if you find a way to engage them during the initial session. My wish is that this book will assist you in this endeavor. I hope your therapeutic ride with adolescents is not too bumpy and that your journey is ultimately satisfying.

# Notes

## Foreword

1. Kleinke, 1994, p. 176.
2. Heaton, 1998, p. 69.

## Chapter One

1. Richards, Abell, & Petersen, 1993.
2. Paikoff & Brooks-Gunn, 1991.
3. Holmbeck & Updegrove, 1995.
4. Dreyer, 1982.
5. Robinson, Ziss, Ganza, Katz, & Robinson, 1991.
6. Miller & Moore, 1990.
7. Sellers, McGraw, & McKinlay, 1994.
8. Children's Defense Fund, 1993.
9. National Institute on Drug Abuse, 1993.
10. McAlister, Perry, & Maccoby, 1979.
11. National Institute on Drug Abuse, 1995.
12. Stephenson, Henry, & Robinson, 1996.
13. Leshner, 1995.
14. See note 11.

15. AAP Committee on Adolescence, 1987.

16. Piaget, 1972.

17. Elkind, 1967.

18. Elkind, 1985.

19. Elkind, 1984.

20. Simmons, Burgeson, Carlton-Ford, & Blyth, 1987.

21. Stark, 1990.

22. Petti, 1978.

23. Diamond & Siqueland, 1995.

24. Erikson, 1968.

25. Spencer & Markstrom-Adams, 1990.

26. Marcia, 1980.

27. Gilligan, 1988.

28. Lyons, 1990.

29. Chillman, 1980.

30. Holmbeck & Hill, 1988.

31. Collins, 1990.

32. Laursen & Collins, 1994.

33. See note 3.

34. Berndt, 1979.

35. Steinberg & Silverberg, 1986.

36. Dishion, Andrews, & Crosby, 1995.

37. Offer, Ostrov, & Howard, 1989.

## Chapter Two

1. Achenbach, 1985.

2. Achenbach & Edelbrock, 1981.

3. Holmbeck & Updegrove, 1995.

4. Rutter, 1985.

5. See note 3, p. 28.

6. Sheehan, Sheehan, & Minichiello, 1981.

7. Rapoport, et al., 1981.

8. Wenar, 1989.

9. Conger & Peterson, 1984.

10. Siegel & Griffin, 1983.

11. Carlson, 1981.

12. Hudgens, 1974.

13. Kestenbaum, 1980.

14. Shaffer, 1985.

15. Shaffi, Carrigan, Whittinghill, & Derrick, 1985.

16. Petti & Larson, 1987.

17. Doctors, 1981.

18. Stewart, deBlois, & Cummings, 1980.

19. Ullman, Barkley, & Brown, 1978.

20. Barkley, 1981.

21. Gittelman, Mannuzza, Shenker, & Bonagura, 1985.

22. Achenbach & Edelbrock, 1978.

23. Lewis, Lewis, Unger, & Goldman, 1984.

24. Puig-Antich, 1982.

25. Moore, Chamberlain, & Mukai, 1979.

26. Margolis, 1995.

27. Garner & Garfinkel, 1980.

28. Crowther, Post, & Zaynor, 1985; Katzman, Wolchik, & Braver, 1984.

29. Smart, Beaumont, & George, 1976.

30. Muuss, 1986.

31. Gilchrist & Schinke, 1983.

32. Patterson, 1995.

33. Savin-Williams, 1996.

34. See note 33, p. 153.

35. Martin & Hetrick, 1988.

36. See note 33, p. 168.

37. Martin, 1982.

38. Savin-Williams, 1994.

39. See note 33.

40. Davidson & Baum, 1986.

## Chapter Three

1. Jackson-Gilfort & Liddle, 1998.

## Chapter Four

1. Horvath & Greenberg (Eds.), 1994; Tramotana, 1980.

2. Liddle, 1995.

3. Sommers-Flanagan & Sommers-Flanagan, 1995.

4. Canino & Spurlock, 1994.

5. Baumrind, 1991.

## Chapter Five

1. Minuchin, 1974.

2. See note 1.

3. Rusk, 1971.

4. Boyd-Franklin, 1989.

## Chapter Six

1. Thompson & Gustafson, 1996.

2. Sweeten, 1997.

3. Ammerman, Van Hasselt, & Hersen, 1987.

4. Anderson, Clarke, & Spain, 1982; Jan, Freeman, & Scott, 1977; Van Hasselt & Hersen, 1987.

5. Gottman, Gonso, & Rasmussen, 1975.

6. See note 5.

7. Hollingsworth, 1942, p. 45.

8. Delisle, 1984.

9. Lerner, 1993; Platt & Olson, 1997.

10. See note 9.

11. Feagans, 1983; Mercer, 1991.

12. Shaywitz & Shaywitz, 1991; Silver, 1990.

13. See note 9; Geisthardt & Munsch, 1996.

14. Huntington & Bebder, 1993.

15. Bray, 1988; Bray & Hetherington, 1993.

16. See note 15.

17. Hetherington, 1993; Hetherington & Clingempeel, 1992.

18. Bray & Harvey, 1995.

19. See note 18.

20. Lee, 1997.

21. Ramirez, 1991.

22. Hsu, 1983; LaFromboise & Low, 1989; Watkins, 1990.

23. Paniagua, 1994; Vraniak & Pickett, 1993.

# References

AAP Committe on Adolescence (1987).

Achenbach, T. M. (1985). *Assessment and taxonomy of child and adolescent psychopathology: Vol. 3. Developmental clinical psychology and psychiatry.* Thousand Oaks, CA: Sage.

Achenbach, T. M., & Edelbrock, C. S. (1978). The classification of child psychopathology: A review and analysis of empirical efforts. *Psychological Bulletin, 85,* 1275–1301.

Achenbach, T. M., & Edelbrock, C. S. (1981). Behavioral problems and competencies reported by parents of normal and disturbed children aged four to sixteen. *Monographs of the Society for Research in Child Development, 46* (Serial No. 188).

Ammerman, R. T., Van Hasselt, V. B., & Hersen, M. (1987). The handicapped adolescent. In V. B. Van Hasselt & M. Hersen (Eds.), *Handbook of adolescent psychology* (pp. 413–422). New York: Pergamon Press.

Anderson, E. M., Clarke, L., & Spain, B. (1982). *Disability in adolescence.* London: Methuen.

Barkley, R. A. (1981). *Hyperactive children: A handbook for diagnosis and treatment.* New York: Guilford Press.

Baumrind, D. (1991). The influence of parenting styles on adolescent competence and substance abuse. *Journal of Early Adolescence, 11,* 56–95.

Berndt, T. (1979). Developmental changes in conformity to peers and parents. *Developmental Psychology, 15,* 608–617.

Boyd-Franklin, N. (1989). *Black families in therapy.* New York: Guilford Press.

Bray, J. H. (1988). Children's development during early remarriage. In E. M. Hetherington & J. Arasteh (Eds.), *The impact of divorce, single-parenting and step-parenting on children* (pp. 279–298). Hillsdale, NJ: Erlbaum.

Bray, J. H., & Harvey, D. H. (1995). Adolescents in stepfamilies: Developmental family interventions. *Psychotherapy, 32,* 122–130.

Bray, J. H., & Hetherington, E. M. (1993). Families in transition: Introduction and overview. *Journal of Family Psychology, 7*, 3–8.

Canino, I., & Spurlock, J. (1994). *Culturally diverse children and adolescents: Assessment, diagnosis, and treatment.* New York: Guilford Press.

Carlson, G. (1981). The phenomenology of adolescent depression. *Adolescent Psychiatry, 9*, 411–421.

Children's Defense Fund (1993). Birth to teens. *CDF Reports, 0276-6531.*

Chillman, C.W. (1980). *Adolescent sexuality in a changing American society*: Social and psychological perspectives (NIH Publication No. 80-1426). Bethesda, MD: National Institutes of Health.

Collins, W. A. (1990). Parent-child relationships in transition to adolescence: Continuity and change in interaction, affect, and cognition. In R. Montemayor, G. R. Adams, & T. P. Gugliotta (Eds.), *From childhood to adolescence: A transitional period?* Thousand Oaks, CA: Sage.

Conger, J. J., & Peterson, A. C. (1984). *Adolescence and youth: Psychological development in a changing world.* New York: HarperCollins.

Crowther, J. H., Post, G., & Zaynor, L. (1985). The prevalence of bulimia and binge eating in adolescent girls. *International Journal of Eating Disorders, 4*(1), 29–42.

Davidson, L. M., & Baum, A. (1986). Chronic stress and post-traumatic stress disorder. *Journal of Consulting and Clinical Psychology, 54*, 303–308.

Delisle, J. R. (1984). *Gifted children speak out.* New York: Walker.

Diamond, G., & Siqueland, L. (1995). Family therapy for the treatment of depressed adolescents. *Psychotherapy, 32*, 77–90.

Dishion, T. J., Andrews, D. W., & Crosby, L. (1995). Antisocial boys and their friends in early adolescence: Relationship characteristics, quality, and interactional process. *Child Development, 66*, 139–151.

Doctors, S. (1981). The symptom of delicate self-cutting in adolescent females: A developmental view. In S. C. Feinstein, J. G. Looney, A. Z. Schwartzberg, & A. D. Sorosky (Eds.), *Adolescent psychiatry* (pp. 443–460). Chicago: University of Chicago Press.

Dreyer, P. H. (1982). Sexuality during adolescence. In B. B. Wolman (Ed.), *Handbook of developmental psychology.* Englewood Cliffs, NJ: Prentice Hall.

Elkind, D. (1967). Egocentrism in adolescence. *Child Development, 38*, 1025–1034.

Elkind, D. (1984). *All grown up and no place to go.* Reading, MA: Addison-Wesley.

Elkind, D. (1985). Egocentrism redux. *Developmental Review, 5*, 218–226.

Erikson, E. (1968). *Identity: Youth and crisis.* New York: Norton.

Feagans, L. (1983). A current review of leaning disabilities. *Journal of Pediatrics, 5*, 487–493.

Garner, D. M., & Garfinkel, P. E. (1980). Sociocultural factors in the development of anorexia nervosa. *Psychological Medicine, 10*, 647–656.

Geisthardt, C., & Munsch, J. (1996). Coping with school stress: A comparison of adolescents with and without learning disabilities. *Journal of Learning Disabilities*, 287–296.

Gilchrist, L. D., & Schinke, S. P. (1983). Counseling with adolescents about their sexuality. In C. S. Chilman (Ed.), *Adolescent sexuality in a changing American society* (pp. 230–250). New York: Wiley.

Gilligan, C. (1988). Exit-voice dilemmas in adolescent development. In C. Gilligan, J. V. Ward, J. M. Taylor, & B. Bardige (Eds.), *Mapping the moral domain*. Cambridge, MA: Harvard University Press.

Gittelman, R., Mannuzza, S., Shenker, R., & Bonagura, N. (1985). Hyperactive boys almost grown up: 1. Psychiatric status. *Archives of General Psychiatry, 42*, 937–947.

Gottman, J., Gonso, J., & Rasmussen, B. (1975). Social interaction, social competence, and friendship in children. *Child Development, 46*, 709–718.

Heaton, J. A. (1998) Building basic therapeutic skills (p. 69). San Francisco: Jossey-Bass.

Hetherington, E. M. (1993). An overview of the Virginia longitudinal study of divorce and remarriage. *Journal of Family Psychology*, 39–56.

Hetherington, E. M., & Clingempeel, W. G. (1992). Coping with marital transitions: A family systems perspective. *Monographs of the Society for Research in Child Development*. No. 1–2, 54.

Hirshoren, A., & Schnittjer, C. (1979). Dimensions of problem behavior in deaf children. *Journal of Abnormal Child Psychology, 7*, 221–228.

Hollingsworth, L. S. (1942). *Children above 180 IQ Stanford Binet: Origin and development*. Yonkers, NY: World Book Company.

Holmbeck, G. N., & Hill, J. P. (1988). Storm and stress beliefs about adolescence: Prevalence, self-reported antecedents, and effects of an undergraduate course. *Journal of Youth and Adolescence, 17*, 285–306.

Holmbeck, G. N., & Updegrove, A. L. (1995). Clinical-developmental interface: Implications of developmental research for adolescent psychotherapy. *Psychotherapy, 32*, 16–33.

Horvath, A. O., & Greenberg, L. S. (Eds.). (1994). *The working alliance: Theory, research, and practice*. New York: Wiley.

Hsu, J. (1983). Asian family interaction patterns and their therapeutic implications. *International Journal of Family Psychiatry, 4*, 307–320.

Hudgens, R. W. (1974). *Psychiatric disorders in adolescence*. Baltimore: Williams & Wilkins.

Huntington, D. J., & Bebder, W. N. (1993). Adolescents with learning disabilities at risk? Emotional well-being, depression, suicide. *Journal of Learning Disabilities*, 159–166.

Jackson-Gilfort, A., & Liddle, H. (1998). Family therapy engagement and culturally relevant theme content for African American adolescent males: Summary of a pilot study. *Family Psychologist*, *15*(2), 6–12.

Jan, J. E., Freeman, R. D., & Scott, E. P. (1977). *Visual impairment in children and adolescents*. Philadelphia: Grune & Stratton.

Katzman, M. A., Wolchik, S. A., & Braver, S. L. (1984). Prevalence of frequent binge eating and bulimia in a nonclinical college sample. *International Journal of Eating Disorders*, *3*, 53–62.

Kestenbaum, C. J. (1980). Adolescents at risk for manic-depressive illness. *Adolescent Psychiatry*, *8*, 344–366.

Kleinke, C. L. (1994). *Common principles of psychotherapy*. Pacific Grove, CA: Brooks/Cole.

LaFromboise, T. E., & Low, W. (1989). American Indian children and adolescents. In J. T. Gibbs & L. N. Huang (Eds.), *Children of color: Psychological interventions with minority youth* (pp. 114–147). San Francisco: Jossey-Bass.

Laursen, B., & Collins, W. A. (1994). Interpersonal conflict during adolescence. *Psychological Bulletin*, *115*, 197–209.

Lee, C. C. (Ed.) (1997). *Multicultural issues in counseling: New approaches to diversity* (2nd ed.). Alexandria, VA: American Counseling Association.

Lerner, J. (1993). *Learning disabilities theories, diagnosis, and teaching strategies* (6th ed.). Boston: Houghton Mifflin.

Leshner, A. I. (1995). *Statement of Alan I. Leshner, Director, National Institute on Drug Abuse, National Institute of Health*. Washington, DC: U.S. Department of Health and Human Services.

Lewis, D. O., Lewis, M., Unger, L., & Goldman, C. (1984). Conduct disorder and its synonyms: Diagnoses of dubious validity and usefulness. *American Journal of Psychiatry*, *141*, 514–519.

Liddle, H. A. (1995). Conceptual and clinical dimensions of a multidimensional, multisystems engagement strategy in family-based adolescent treatment. *Psychotherapy*, *32*, 39–58.

Lyons, N. P. (1990). Listening to voices we have not heard. In C. Gilligan, N. P. Lyons, & T. J. Hammer (Eds.), *Making connections*. Cambridge, MA: Harvard University Press.

Marcia, J. E. (1980). Identity in adolescence. In J. Adelson (Ed.), *Handbook of adolescent psychology* (pp. 159–187). New York: Wiley.

Margolis, R. (1995). Adolescent chemical dependence: Assessment, treatment, and management. *Psychotherapy*, *32*, 172–179.

Martin, A. D. (1982). Learning to hide: The socialization of the gay adolescent. *Adolescent Psychiatry*, *10*, 52–65.

Martin, A. D., & Hetrick, E. S. (1988). The stigmatization of the gay and lesbian adolescent. *Journal of Homosexuality, 15*, 163–183.

McAlister, A. L., Perry, C., & Maccoby, N. (1979). Adolescent smoking: Onset and prevention. *Pediatrics, 63*, 650–658.

Mercer, C. D. (1991). *Students with learning disabilities* (4th ed.). Old Tappan, NJ: MacMillan.

Miller, B. C., & Moore, K. A. (1990). Adolescent sexual behavior, pregnancy, and parenting: Research through the 1980s. *Journal of Marriage and the Family, 52*, 1025–1044.

Minuchin, S. (1974). *Families and family therapy*. Cambridge, MA: Harvard University Press.

Moore, D. R., Chamberlain, P., & Mukai, L. H. (1979). Children at risk for delinquency: A follow-up comparison of aggressive children and children who steal. *Journal of Abnormal Child Psychology, 7*, 345–355.

Muuss, R. E. (1986). Adolescent eating disorder: Bulimia. *Adolescence, 21*, 257–267.

National Institute on Drug Abuse. (1993). *Monitoring the future survey*. Washington, DC: U.S. Government Printing Office.

National Institute on Drug Abuse. (1995). *Monitoring the future survey*. Washington, DC: U.S. Government Printing Office.

Offer, D., Ostrov, E., & Howard, K. I. (1989). Adolescence: What is normal? *American Journal of Diseases of Children, 143*, 731–736.

Paikoff, R. L., & Brooks-Gunn, J. (1991). Do parent-child relationships change during puberty? *Psychological Bulletin, 110*, 47–66.

Paniagua, F. (1994). *Assessing and treating culturally diverse clients: A practical guide*. Thousand Oaks, CA: Sage.

Patterson, C. (1995). Sexual orientation and human development: An overview. *Developmental Psychology, 31*, 3–11.

Petti, T. A. (1978). Depression in hospitalized child psychiatry patients: Approaches to measuring depression. *Journal of the American Academy of Child Psychiatry, 22*, 11–21.

Petti, T. A., & Larson, C. N. (1987). Depression and suicide. In V. Van Hasselt & M. Hersen (Eds.), *Handbook of adolescent psychology* (pp. 288–312). New York: Pergamon Press.

Piaget, J. (1972). Intellectual evolution from adolescence to adulthood. *Human Development, 15*, 1–12.

Platt, D. B., & Olson, J. L. (1997). *Teaching adolescents with mild disabilities*. Pacific Grove, CA: Brooks/Cole.

Puig-Antich, J. (1982). Major depression and conduct disorder in prepuberty. *Journal of the American Academy of Child Psychiatry, 21*, 491–501.

Ramirez, M. (1991). *Psychotherapy and counseling with minorities: A cognitive approach to individual and cultural differences*. New York: Pergamon Press.

Rapoport, J., Elkins, R., Langer, D. H., Sceery, W., Buchsbaum, M. S., Gillin, J. C., Murphy, D. L., Zahn, T. P., Lake, R., Ludlow, C., & Mendelson, W. (1981). Childhood obsessive-compulsive disorders. *American Journal of Psychiatry, 138*, 1545–1554.

Richards, M. H., Abell, S. N., & Petersen, A. C. (1993). Biological development. In P. H. Tolan & B. J. Cohler (Eds.), *Handbook of clinical research and practice with adolescents* (pp. 21–44). New York: Wiley.

Robinson, I., Ziss, K., Ganza, B., Katz, S., & Robinson, E. (1991). Twenty years of the sexual revolution, 1965–1985: An update. *Journal of Marriage and the Family, 53*, 216–220.

Rusk, T. (1971). Opportunity and technique in crisis psychiatry. *Comprehensive Psychiatry, 12*, 249–263.

Rutter, M. (1985, July). *Some notes on psychopathology in adolescence*. Invited presentation at the Adolescence and Adolescent Development workshop sponsored by the Committee on Child Development Research and Public Policy, National Academy of Sciences, Woods Hole, MA.

Savin-Williams, R. C. (1994). Verbal and physical abuse as stressors in the lives of sexual minority youth: Associations with school problems, running away, substance abuse, prostitution, and suicide. *Journal of Counseling and Clinical Psychology, 62*, 261–264.

Savin-Williams, R. C. (1996). Ethnic-and sexual-minority youth. In R. C. Savin-Williams & K. M. Cohen (Eds.), *The lives of lesbians, gays, and bisexuals: Children to adults* (pp. 152–165). Orlando: Harcourt Brace.

Sellers, D. E., McGraw, S. A., & McKinlay, J. B. (1994). Does the promotion and distribution of condoms increase teen sexual activity? Evidence from an HIV prevention program for Latino youth. *American Journal of Public Health, 84*, 1952–1959.

Shaffer, D. (1985). Depression, mania, and suicidal acts. In M. Rutter & L. Hersov (Eds.), *Child and adolescent psychiatry: Modern approaches* (2nd ed., pp. 698–719). Oxford, England: Blackwell Scientific Publications.

Shaffi, M., Carrigan, S., Whittinghill, J. R., & Derrick, A. (1985). Psychological autopsy of completed suicide in children and adolescents: A comparative study. *American Journal of Psychiatry, 142*, 1061–1064.

Shaywitz, S. E., & Shaywitz, B. A. (1991). Introduction to the special series on attention deficit disorder. *Journal of Learning Disabilities, 24*, 68–71.

Sheehan, D. V., Sheehan, K. E., & Minichiello, W. E. (1981). Age of onset of phobic disorders: A reevaluation. *Comprehensive Psychiatry, 6*, 544–553.

Siegel, L. J., & Griffin, N. J. (1983). Adolescents' concepts of depression among their peers. *Adolescence, 8*, 965–973.

Silver, L. B. (1990). Attention deficit-hyperactivity disorder: Is it a learning disability or a related disorder? *Journal of Learning Disabilities, 23*, 32–37.

Simmons, R. G., Burgeson, R., Carlton-Ford, S., & Blyth, D. A. (1987). The impact of cumulative change in early adolescence. *Child Development, 58,* 1220–1234.

Smart, D. E., Beaumont, P. J., & George, G. C. (1976). Some personality characteristics of patients with anorexia nervosa. *British Journal of Psychiatry, 128,* 57–60.

Sommers-Flanagan, J., & Sommers-Flanagan, R. (1995). Psychotherapeutic techniques with treatment-resistant adolescents. *Psychotherapy, 32,* 131–140.

Spencer, M. B., & Markstrom-Adams, C. (1990). Identity processes among racial and ethnic minority children. *Child Development, 61,* 290–310.

Stark, K. (1990). *Childhood depression: School-based intervention.* New York: Guilford Press.

Steinberg, L., & Silverberg, S. B. (1986). Influences on marital satisfaction during the middle stages of the family life cycle. *Journal of Marriage and the Family, 49,* 751–760.

Stephenson, A. L., Henry, C. S., & Robinson, L. C. (1996). Family characteristics and adolescent substance abuse. *Adolescence, 31,* 59–77.

Stewart, M. A., deBlois, C. S., & Cummings, C. (1980). Psychiatric disorder in the parents of hyperactive boys and those with conduct disorders. *Journal of Child Psychology and Psychiatry, 21,* 283–292.

Sweeten, K. K. (1997). *Developmental issues for male adolescents with Tourette's syndrome.* Unpublished doctoral dissertation, California School of Professional Psychology, San Diego.

Thompson, R. J., & Gustafson, K. E. (1996). *Adaptation to chronic childhood illness.* Washington, DC: American Psychological Association.

Tramotana, M. C. (1980). Critical review of research on psychotherapy outcome with adolescents: 1967–1977. *Psychological Bulletin, 88,* 429–450.

Ullman, D. G., Barkley, R. A., & Brown, H. W. (1978). The behavioral symptoms of hyperkinetic children who successfully responded to stimulant drug treatment. *American Journal of Orthopsychiatry, 48,* 425–437.

Van Hasselt, V. B., & Hersen, M. (1987). *Handbook of adolescent psychology.* New York: Pergamon Press.

Vraniak, D., & Pickett, S. (1993). Improving interventions with American ethnic minority children: Recurrent and recalcitrant challenges. In T. Kratochwill & R. Morris (Eds.), *Handbook of psychotherapy with children and adolescents* (pp. 502–540). Needham Heights, MA: Allyn & Bacon.

Watkins, C. E. (1990). The effects of counselor self-disclosure: A research review. *Counseling Psychologist, 18,* 477–500.

Wenar, C. (1989). *Developmental psychopathology from infancy through adolescence.* New York: Random House.

# The Author

*Neil Ribner, Ph.D.*, is an associate professor and associate director of the Clinical Psy. D. program at the California School of Professional Psychology (CSPP) in San Diego, where he has been on the core faculty for over twenty years. At CSPP, Ribner is also coordinator of family and child training, the director of the Family Track, and the director of the Family Center, an outpatient clinic specializing in the treatment of families and in conducting court-ordered custody evaluations.

In addition to his responsibilities at CSPP, Ribner has served on the California division of the National Committee on Youth Suicide Prevention, the California state division of the Stepfamily Association of America, and the San Diego Juvenile Court Peer Review Committee. He has also been on the Education and Training Committee of the American Psychological Association's Division of Family Psychology and the San Diego Psychological Association's Ethics and Standards Committee.

Ribner lives in San Diego with his wife of twenty-eight years and his fourteen-year-old son; he has two older children away at college.

# Index